To my husband, who is the best business partner and partner in life. Thank you for supporting and encouraging my work, and for making lots of fresh homemade juices with me.

Contents

Introduction

Welcome to the Plant-Powered Juicing Plan! I am thrilled that you are taking time to care for your health and well-being. I hope this book allows you to discover how truly incredible plants are for nourishing your body and mind, and that you will fall in love with fruits and vegetables in a whole new way. Freshly made juice is one of my favorite ways to consume more fruits and veggies, which is why I've devoted an entire book to celebrating juice.

So what is juicing? Technically, juicing is a process of extracting the liquid from plant matter, such as fruits and vegetables. To achieve this, you need to be really strong! Just kidding—juice requires a juicer, and a blended juice requires a blender. One cup of juice can often contain the nutrition of 10 cups of fruits and vegetables, which is a powerful way to saturate your body with nutrients. In the chapters to come, we'll explore the benefits of juicing, juicing versus blending, equipment options, and more.

Because freshly squeezed juice is so nutrient-dense, it's a great way to help us meet, and exceed, our recommended daily intake of fruits and veggies. In fact, the 2015–2020 USDA Dietary Guidelines for Americans recommends that fruits and vegetables make up half our plate, and with good reason. The nutrients in fruits and vegetables are necessary for the optimal functioning of every system in the body and are associated with a reduced risk of chronic diseases. Fruits and vegetables are also relatively low in calories, replacing high-calorie foods that can cause weight gain. The organization Fruits & Veggies More Matters states that, "Fruits and vegetables are major contributors of a number of nutrients that are underconsumed in the U.S. such as vitamins A, C, and K, potassium, fiber and magnesium."

I started juicing as a way to improve my energy levels and nourish my body. As a business owner and entrepreneur, I wear many hats, and soon realized that it's easy to feel run-down. Like many people, I fell in love with the power of coffee as fuel. I even worked in a coffee shop in college, where I learned the history of coffee and how to make a fabulous espresso. I was hooked! I could easily enjoy one or two cups of coffee in the morning and then another cup in the afternoon, or maybe a latte, depending mood. While I loved coffee, I did not feel great about my dependency. If I didn't have my morning coffee, I felt tired, inefficient, and pretty grumpy. If I didn't get my afternoon latte, I would get a headache and experience a major energy slump. I also started to notice that my love for coffee meant I was not drinking enough water. My skin was dry, and I was breaking out in acne. While coffee helped me get through stressful workdays, it was also taxing my adrenal glands (glands that produce important hormones), which left me feeling even more exhausted.

Oh, I still love coffee! Thankfully, coffee beans are packed with antioxidants and can fit into a healthy lifestyle. However, I no longer depend on it or need it as urgently as I did. I still enjoy one cup of a hot caffeinated beverage like coffee or tea on most days, but now it's more about the experience. I mindfully enjoy a small cup of coffee or make a matcha latte with coconut milk. Today, I am all about balance and moderation, not deprivation, which is a key philosophy for a healthy food-and-body relationship.

And this leads us to juicing. I started drinking juice and blended juices (see Juicing versus Blending, page 5) in an attempt to replace my afternoon cup of coffee. Almost immediately, I noticed how much better I felt. One of the signs of dehydration is mental fog, and *wow*, does juicing lift that fog. All the fruits and veggies in juices are energizing and surprisingly filling, especially when in a blended juice, which we'll talk more about throughout this book.

Now, I drink at least one giant green drink every day. Over the years, juicing has continued to improve my health, and my skin, hair, and digestive system have all benefited from juices and blended juices. This is why I am so excited to share this book with you. I hope that you, too, find that juicing improves your health and helps you achieve your wellness goals, which may include weight loss.

This book will equip you with knowledge of the power of plants to help you thrive and feel your best. We'll explore how juicing can help you achieve your health goals. You'll learn how to confidently shop for produce, pick out a juicer, and make nourishing juices, blended juices, and even plant-based main dishes.

Also included is a 5-Day Plant-Powered Juicing Plan, designed to nourish your body so you feel your absolute best. You'll drink a combination of fresh juice and blended juices, and of course enjoy some plant-based recipes, too, because crunching and munching is an important part of feeling satisfied.

Juicing is a wonderful complement to a healthy lifestyle. The 5-Day Plant-Powered Juicing Plan is not a diet, nor is its goal deprivation. It is about adding to your life: Adding more fruits, vegetables, and plant-based ingredients so you feel your very best. Because nutrition is not one-size-fits-all, I invite you to adjust the type and quantity of ingredients in the plan so it works best for you and your specific dietary needs.

Are you ready to power your body with plants, sip on amazing tasty juices, and watch the magic of fruits and veggies enhance your health, boost your energy, and lift your mood? Let's get started!

PART ONE
Juicing for a More Vibrant You

1

Why Juice?

Juicing is an excellent way to hydrate and nourish your body with vitamins, minerals, enzymes, anti-oxidants, and phytonutrients. Many of us, juggling hectic schedules and multiple responsibilities, find it difficult to consume all the produce we need. Juicing can easily help us meet, and even exceed, our recommended intake of plants. Your body quickly absorbs the nutrients, which means that fresh juice can help you feel better, both in the short and long term!

What is Juicing?

When we think of juice, many of us may think of store-bought apple juice or orange juice. Unfortunately, many store-bought juice options are pasteurized at high temperatures, which can denature nutrients. Store-bought juice may also contain added sugar. Fresh juice, however, is continuing to gain popularity for its taste and myriad health benefits. It really is unlike any other beverage in terms of the potential density of nutrients in every sip. People are turning to juice for a number of reasons: It's a simple, tasty treat; it provides a great energy boost; and it's an effective part of a purposeful health and healing plan.

Juicing is the process of extracting liquid from the pulp (fiber) of produce to create hydrating, nutrient-dense, colorful liquid. The process also produces pulp, which has its own value, and I'll share how to repurpose the pulp in fun and delicious ways. There are various juicing methods and equipment options, which are covered in later chapters. Whether you pick up your juice from a local juice shop or make it yourself, know that fresh juice is a great way to provide your body with the nutrients essential for growth, health, and feeling your best.

The Plant-Powered Juicing Plan

By "juice diet," you may anticipate that the only source of nutrition you'll consume is from juice. While a juice-only cleanse can be beneficial for some people, especially those with particular health concerns, a juice-only plan is not necessary in order to benefit from the power of juice.

Juice is the unmistakable hero in this plan, but the mission is to nourish you, not make you feel deprived or have you follow a plan that is unrealistic for your lifestyle. On the contrary, the plan features varied, simple recipes packed with nutrients that will keep you feeling full and fresh. Throughout the five days, you'll enjoy a mix of fresh juice, blended juice, and plant-powered snacks and meals. As you progress, get ready to notice a marked increase in your physical energy and mental clarity.

JUICING VERSUS BLENDING

Juicing and blending offer two ways to drink your way to optimum health. Each comes with its own benefits. Let's explore the differences between the two methods, and what they can do for you.

JUICING

The juicing process extracts the liquid from the pulp (fiber) of produce. Juicing has many benefits.

- High quantities of nutrients are absorbed from the produce.
- Nutrients are quickly absorbed into the bloodstream.
- Juice is gentle for those with digestive troubles.

BLENDING

Freshly made blended juices or smoothies are made from entire, whole ingredients. This process keeps the fiber intact. Blended juice benefits include:

- Fiber boosts satiety and keeps you feeling full for longer.
- Fiber is ideal for those monitoring blood sugar levels.
- Fiber supports digestive health and bowel regularity.
- Protein powder and supplements can be added to further boost flavor and nutrition.

Many of the juice recipes in this book can be blended instead of juiced to retain the fiber. This is just one of the many ways you can customize the plan so it works for you!

On each day of the Plant-Powered Juicing Plan, you'll consume two juices, one blended juice, one super-simple snack, and one plant-powered supper.

You'll start each morning with a fresh juice for breakfast, followed by a mid-morning snack. For lunch, you'll enjoy a fiber-packed blended juice to keep you feeling full. In the afternoon, you'll have another fresh juice as an energy boost, happy-hour elixir, or "cleanse the day away" beverage before dinner. Each evening, you can look forward to a tasty and comforting plant-powered supper.

During the five days, I recommend eliminating caffeine and alcohol. One goal of the plan is to give your system a rest from stimulants, which can be addictive and dehydrating. Caffeine and alcohol are also acidic (pro-inflammatory), which, in our pursuit of optimal health, is something we want to minimize. Instead, for just five full days, your main source of energy and nutrition will come from fresh plants via juices, blended juices, and healthy meals. To set yourself up for success, begin minimizing your intake of caffeine and alcohol for a week or two before starting the plan.

That said, a healthy lifestyle is about progress, not perfection. You may stumble, and if you do, don't beat yourself up—new habits need time to take root! Also, be flexible with your mindset. Depending on your lifestyle and schedule, you can switch up when you consume each meal and snack, keeping with the same theme of two juices, one blended juice, one snack, and one meal per day.

As with any lifestyle change, you may find that the first day or two are the most difficult, especially if you regularly consume a diet high in caffeine, alcohol, or sugar. Withdrawal symptoms such as headaches may occur. This is one reason I recommend minimizing those foods before you begin the plan. However, to combat symptoms of withdrawal, make sure you stay hydrated. Juice is exceptionally hydrating, but it's also important to drink filtered water between meals. Because this plan is not a calorie-deficit plan, but a nourishment plan, once you get rolling you may notice an energy boost that you used to count on coffee or sugar to provide—*hooray*! Keeping busy with productive activities can also smooth the transition. Gift yourself with a brisk walk outside, gentle yoga, stretches, or meditation.

If the idea of the plan seems overwhelming, why not take a few weeks to prepare physically and mentally? Write down a few reasons this plan interests you. What health goals do you wish to achieve? And how can the plan move you closer to those goals? Having a meaningful reason to follow the plan can excite and motivate you. Take advantage of the daily journal portion of this book (page 52) to note your thoughts, feelings, and reflections as you start your journey.

The more prepared you are, the more enjoyable and successful the plan will likely be. Other preparations I recommend taking before you start are to increase your water intake and reduce your intake of processed foods, especially those with added sugar (in addition to the already-mentioned elimination of alcohol and caffeine). Talk with your friends or family about the plan, and invite them to join you. Having a juice buddy is a fun way to share the experience through encouragement and support. Finally, go ahead and test out some of the recipes before you even begin the plan!

The Benefits of the Plant-Powered Juicing Plan

There are so many rewarding benefits to juicing and consuming a diet rich in plant-based foods. As you begin this plan and increase your daily intake of juice and plants, you may notice some (or all!) of these benefits.

Energy Boost

Chronic fatigue can be the result of many factors, including stress, dehydration, poor sleep, hormone imbalance, and insufficient nutrition. Juice hydrates and provides an incredible amount and breadth of nutrients, giving the body and brain what it needs to thrive. Fresh juice is nature's energy drink!

Healthy Weight

Healthy weight loss is more complicated than "calories in and calories out." Clearly, nutrition and exercise play a role in healthy weight maintenance, but so do stress, genetics, health conditions, lifestyle, and medication. That said, this plan is a nourishment plan, not a weight-loss plan—and hopefully the catalyst to a simple and positive lifestyle adjustment. However, you may notice that when you are consuming a diet consisting of real, whole, plant-based foods, you feel better and have more energy, which makes it easier to want to eat well and exercise. A plant-based diet is also a nutrient-dense diet, which supports the optimal functioning of every cell and organ in your body. Even if weight loss is your goal, this plan can provide a wonderful foundation to help you achieve and maintain a healthy weight in a natural, balanced, and nourishing way.

Better Bowel Movements

While juices lack fiber, the blended juice and plant-powered meals in this plan balance the scales with loads of fiber. Some studies show that the average American only consumes 15 grams of fiber per day. The recommended daily intake of fiber is 25 to 35 grams, which this plan handily exceeds. Bowel health is critically important for overall health, as it's one of the body's main vehicles for cleansing and eliminating toxins. According to the Mayo Clinic, a high-fiber diet may normalize bowel movements, help maintain bowel health, lower cholesterol, help control blood sugar levels, and support a healthy weight. Two key elements for healthy bowel movements are proper hydration and sufficient fiber, both of which you'll easily achieve on this plan.

Diminished Bloating

What can I say—occasional gas and bloating are a part of life. For women in particular, hormone fluctuations are a natural part of the monthly cycle and can result in gas or bloating at certain times of the month, regardless of diet. However, if you struggle with daily gas, bloating, heartburn, or irritable bowel syndrome, your gut and digestive system are sending the message that they're not happy. One culprit can be irregular bowel movements, and this plan can improve that. Another key to banish belly bloat is a happy, healthy gut, so read on for more on this important benefit.

Restored Gut Health

Almost two thousand years ago, Hippocrates (one of the most highly regarded pioneers in medical history) stated, "All disease begins in the gut." Humbling knowledge as we fast-forward to the twenty-first century, in which we are still learning about the complexity and power of the gastrointestinal system and its role in overall health. The gastrointestinal system, otherwise known as "the gut," plays a variety of crucial roles, much beyond digesting food to use as energy.

A 2013 study focusing on gut bacteria in health and disease stated, "A new era in medical science has dawned with the realization of the critical role of the 'forgotten organ,' the gut microbiota, in health and disease." The article explains that with this new information comes the increased aware- ness of the potential health benefits of intentionally modifying the gut flora. To that end, plant-based foods are packed with nutrients that can modify, heal, and restore the gut. This book features many gut-healthy recipes, and none contain common dietary allergens—such as wheat, gluten, dairy, and soy—that may aggravate the gut. If you have additional food allergens, please feel free to alter this plan to suit your dietary needs.

Hydration

Signs of dehydration include a slow and sluggish metabolism, impaired decision-making abilities, brain fog, achy joints, digestive troubles, inabil- ity to flush out toxins and waste—to name just a few. Because the body is predominantly made of water, proper hydration is key for overall health. Fresh and blended juices hydrate and nourish the body at the same time—it's a two-for-one benefits package!

Natural Detoxification

We are all exposed daily to both avoidable and unavoidable toxins. The word "toxin" may sound trendy, and in a sense this is true because with new indus- tries and technologies the chemicals in our air, ground, and water sources are becoming more complex. But toxins have been around for a long time, and we continue to learn more about them. A toxin is simply a substance that damages the body and affects health on a cellular level through oxidation or inflammation. Think of pesticides in food, toxins in water (chlorine, lead, mercury), chemicals in personal-care and home-cleaning products, and pollutants in the air (mold, mildew, exhaust fumes). Long-term, daily exposure to these invisible culprits may result in toxic overload, causing symptoms that may include chronic fatigue, headaches, accelerated aging, achy joints, brain fog, insomnia, and various skin issues. In one study, researchers found an average of 200 industrial chemicals and pollutants in umbilical cord blood from 10 babies born in August and September of 2004 in US hospitals. Tests revealed a total of 287 chemicals in the group. The umbilical cord blood harbored pesticides, consumer-product ingredients, and wastes from burning coal, gasoline, and garbage.

This study reveals the alarming ability of toxins to be stored in the body (commonly in fat cells) and even passed on from mother to baby. Though this is sobering information, the good news is that we have a built-in detoxification machine: the liver. The liver is the body's main detox organ, and it does an extraordinary job helping rid the body of toxins. But like any machine, the liver requires fuel, and what it likes is a variety of vitamins, minerals, enzymes, and antioxidants to allow it to do its job properly. Fresh juice is a concentrated source of these vital nutrients, and the plan in this book has thoughtfully considered all the nutrition necessary to support your body in naturally cleansing and detoxifying on a daily basis.

Proper pH Balance and Inflammation Mitigation

Interesting fact: The human body prefers to remain in a slightly alkaline state of 7.35 to 7.45 pH. The foods we eat can have either an alkaline or acidic effect on the body once consumed. Too much acidity, on the other hand, promotes inflammation. Inflammation within the body may be associated with heart and kidney disease, diabetes, osteoporosis, suppressed immune function, fatigue, and weight gain. Diet plays a huge role in pH balance. Fresh juice provides a concentrated source of alkaline-promoting foods.

TO CLEANSE OR NOT?

People are increasingly turning to juice cleanses (in which the only source of nutrition is juice) in order to detoxify the body, lose weight, increase nutrition consumption, or just feel better. Depending on your state of health, you may benefit from a juice-only cleanse for a short period of time. However, the best way to determine if a juice-only cleanse is right for you is to discuss it with your primary care provider or registered dietitian. If your health care provider approves, together you can create a customized plan, taking into account your overall health and dietary needs. This book can serve as a resource and guide.

It's important to note that a juice-only plan may not be for everyone. If you are pregnant, breastfeeding, or underweight, or if you have a serious health condition, a juice-only plan may not be right for you.

The plan in this book is designed to be suitable for a wide range of individuals. Juice is the star, but we've included some incredible sidekick meals and snacks to keep you feeling full and satisfied. Because the plan includes a mix of fresh juice, blended juice, and whole foods, it is balanced, nutritious, and satisfying. Technically, this is a cleanse plan because it's packed with so much nutrition. You'll be consuming a variety of nutrients that will help your detox organs naturally cleanse on a daily basis, leaving you with only the "good stuff," so you can function at your best.

2

Juicing at Home

Juice shops are wonderful—but buying juice from a shop wasn't a realistic everyday option for me. That's why I learned to make tasty juice at home. It has saved time and money, and what's more, I can juice in my pajamas! In this chapter, I share tips on how to become a home-juicing pro. You'll learn how to pick the right juicer, which tools are essential, how to choose and store produce, and more. After reading this chapter, I hope you'll feel confident and inspired to start juicing on a regular basis.

Choosing a Juicer

There are juicers and then there are *juicers*. When you think of one, you may picture that citrus juicer with a spinning cone that you can press half an orange against to extract the juice. The juicers used for the recipes in this book are a different breed. They are more versatile. They allow you to feed the food through the press and extract the juice—and you're not restricted to citrus. You can feed your juicer with a carrot, cucumber, some ginger, and whatever else! The juicer separates the juice from the pulp, and you can use both in different ways—no waste!

There are a variety of great juicer options available. The best juicer is the one that works for your budget, time, and kitchen space. I recommend picking a quality juicer for optimal yield and nutrition, although you do not have to buy a top-of-the-line juicer to reap the benefits.

Budget. How much does a juicer cost? There's no denying that quality juicers are an investment. A cheaper, lower-quality juicer may yield lower-quality juice in taste, texture, and nutritional value. A bad first date with your juicer may have you not come back—and I want you to have the best experience possible! That said, there are four main types of juicers, which I've outlined in the table on page 16. The table illustrates the differences in cost as well as the pros and cons of each type. From there, you can identify the best one for you.

Time. Let's be real: Fresh juice is not fast food, but, like anything good, it's worth the effort. If you're new to juicing, it may seem a bit overwhelming and time-consuming. But as you get the hang of it, you'll find systems that make juicing more efficient—I'll share some tips later in this chapter.

- **The type of juicer you select can save you time by extending your juice's shelf life.** Higher-quality juicers run at a lower speed, which preserves nutritional value, and which means your juice will last longer. Depending on the juicer you choose, you can juice in advance and keep your creations stored in the refrigerator, ready to go, for up to 3 days.

- **Another time-eater is cleanup.** The more functions your juicer has, the more it can do for you, but, alas, the more pieces there will be to clean!

Space. If there's no convenient place for your juicer to perch, it's not as likely to become part of your daily routine. We all know the saying, "Out of sight out of mind." Before buying a juicer, review your kitchen space and pick your juicer size accordingly.

Juice quality and shelf life. Juicers have a chute through which fruits and veggies travel to meet the press or grinder that extracts the juice from the pulp. Juicers with a high revolution per minute (RPM) generate foam, which results in air bubbles that oxidize the juice, resulting in a shorter shelf life. This is why the recipes in this book direct you to drink your juice within one hour of juicing, to get maximum benefit from the nutrients. Cold-press juicers have a low RPM, which helps retain the juice's nutrients and increases shelf life. With low-RPM juicers, you can prep and store fresh juice in the refrigerator for later.

TYPES OF JUICERS

CENTRIFUGAL JUICER

COST: $75 to $100 range for quality centrifugal juicer

DESCRIPTION: A common type of juicer that chops and grinds produce into pulp and then spins at a high speed to separate juice from the pulp

Large feeder tube on some models can take whole carrots and apples

BEST FOR: Those new to juicing or those who don't want to spend too much money on a higher-end machine

PROS
- Affordable
- Wide mouth to feed fruits and veggies through means less prep work

CONS
- Noisy
- High speed and high RPM creates heat and foam that can oxidize and denature nutrients
- Less juice extracted from pulp
- Unable to juice wheatgrass or leafy greens very well
- Juice must be enjoyed within 1 hour

MASTICATING JUICER

COST: On average $200 to $500

DESCRIPTION: Known as a cold-press juicer because the juicer has a low RPM and does not produce heat. A single auger rotates to crush produce into pulp and squeezes out the juice

BEST FOR: The juicing purist who wants high yield, high nutritional quality, and a quiet juicer

This juicer is versatile and can make baby food, sauces, sorbets, and ice cream

PROS
- Quiet
- Low RPM
- Extracts more juice
- Retains nutrients better than centrifugal juicers
- Juice can be refrigerated for up to 48 hours
- Can juice wheatgrass and leafy greens

CONS
- Investment
- Requires more time for prep, slow juicing process, and additional cleanup

TWIN-GEAR JUICER

COST: $1,000+

DESCRIPTION: Better and more efficient version of masticating juicer.

Two interlocking gears crush and
grind the produce into pulp and
squeeze out the juice with a higher
pressure than masticating juicers,
creating a higher-quality juice

BEST FOR: Serious juice drinkers

PROS
- Quiet
- Low RPM
- Grinds and presses produce,
  increasing juice yield and quality
- Great for juicing greens and
  wheatgrass
- Retains nutrients better than
  centrifugal and masticating
  varieties
- Juice can be refrigerated for up
  to 72 hours

CONS
- Very expensive
- Takes longer to juice
- Heavy

WHEATGRASS JUICER

COST: $20 to $50

DESCRIPTION: Generally hand-crank
operated. Works well for wheatgrass
and leafy greens as well as some
other produce

BEST FOR: The occasional juice drinker
who does not want to spend too
much money

PROS
- Quiet
- Easily portable
- Inexpensive

CONS
- Very limited in terms of what
  produce they can juice
- Slow
- Hand operated

BLENDING FOR JUICE

 A blended juice is a beverage in which the ingredients are processed in a blender rather than run through a juicer. Blended juices retain all the fiber and pulp of the produce, making them more filling and satisfying than regular juice. For individuals who already have a blender, this type of juice may be a smart starting point.

To get the best results and make a delicious blended juice, pick a recipe that contains a variety of water-dense ingredients such as citrus fruits, romaine lettuce, cucumbers, and apples. I've included a variety of blended juice recipes in this book (labeled "Blended Juice"). I recommend a high-speed blender such as a Vitamix or Blendtec for achieving smooth and creamy blended juices. Lower-quality blenders may yield a chewy beverage as a result of all the pulp. Yes, a high-speed blender is also an investment piece; however, a quality blender is incredibly versatile and, personally speaking, one of my most loved and used kitchen tools. A high-speed blender can also make homemade soups (check out the recipes in this book), smoothies, sauces, nut butters, nut milks, and more.

Special note: Blended drinks can be made the night before and stored in the refrigerator or freezer. Give your beverage a good shake or blend again before enjoying!

Essential Tools

As with any creative pursuit, having the right tools makes the job easier and more fun. Most of the items on this list are things you probably already have in your kitchen; I'm just sharing their uses and desired features as they pertain to the art and science of juicing.

Knife. Second to the juicer itself, a sharp knife is the most important tool you need. Virtually any size or type of knife will work—as long as it's comfortable. I like to use knives with a good rubber grip when prepping for juice, as the procedure inevitably makes for wet, slippery hands. Always make sure your knife is sharp. Surprisingly, a dull knife is a more dangerous knife, especially when used on fruits and vegetables with thick skins.

Cutting board. When choosing a cutting board for juice prep, be mindful of cross-contamination. Since juice is raw (not heated above 115°F, or 46°C) it is very important to use a truly clean cutting board. The best option is to have one cutting board for fruit and vegetable prep and an entirely separate cutting board for meat and fish. If a single cutting board is your only option, make sure you select one that you can easily clean with soap and hot water or safely run through a dishwasher.

Peeler. The skin on fruits and vegetables is often nutrient-rich, although some peels have a bitter taste that can overpower your juice. This is a job for a peeler. You can use any type of peeler; just make sure it's sharp and clean.

Scrub brush. Produce comes from the dirt and dirt can be, well, dirty! A good scrub brush is useful for cleaning your produce, especially really dirty root vegetables like beets. Most fruits and vegetables, particularly organic ones, only require a good scrubbing, as their outer layer contains a lot of nutrients. For food safety, designate a scrub brush specifically for fruits and veggies—don't let anyone use it to scrub your sink!

Strainer. Since juice is served raw, it's crucial to wash away any impurities on your fruits and vegetables before juicing.

TIPS FOR JUICING SUCCESS

1   **Read the manual.** I definitely recommend reading the manual of your juicer before you get started in order to fully understand how your juicer operates, and the purpose of each part.

2   **Don't overload the juicer.** Resist the urge to rush or overload the juicer. If you cram in too many pieces of produce or try and force the produce through too quickly, it can jam. Be patient and use small, thin pieces one at a time.

3   **Make it fit.** Some juicers have a narrow juicing chute, so you'll want to make sure your produce is cut thinly enough to feed through the juicer. For greens, it's helpful to roll, fold, or bunch the greens before feeding them through.

4   **Reuse the pulp!** It may feel like juicing is wasteful because you're left with an abundance of pulp. However, there are many fantastic ways to reuse the pulp, such as making recipes (check out the recipes in this book marked "Made with Juice Pulp"), or using the pulp as compost to nourish your garden.

5   **Aim for green.** If juicing for health is your goal, aim to make your juices mostly greens and herbs, with a small amount of fruit to sweeten them up. If you're watching your blood sugar levels, stick with lower-sugar fruits such as green apples, kiwis, or berries.

6   **Rotate ingredients.** It's normal to find a favorite juice combination and want to stick with it. However, to ensure you provide your body with an array of nutrients, aim to try new ingredients. This will also provide a variety of flavors so you don't get bored.

7 **Choose organic when possible.** Pesticides, herbicides, synthetic fertilizers, and chemicals can end up in your juice if you use conventional produce. When possible, choose organic produce to avoid these unwanted additives (see When to Buy Organic, page 25).

8 **Adjust for taste.** If you're not enjoying the flavor of your juice, include one or two pieces of fruit, such as an apple or orange. Another thing to remember is that your palate and taste buds can change over time. What didn't taste good last year could become this year's favorite!

9 **Cold juice tastes best.** Your juice will likely be at room temperature right after you've finished juicing. I like to put my juice in the refrigerator or freezer for about five minutes to quickly chill it, and then add it to a large glass with lots of ice. Crisp, cold juice tastes best! If you've been drinking room-temperature juice, try it chilled—you'll love how much more refreshing it tastes.

10 **Freeze fruits and veggies.** For blended juices, I recommend freezing produce. In addition to improving the texture of blended juices, freezing will help your fruits and veggies last longer, as well as free up space in your refrigerator. You can chop and freeze broccoli, zucchini, cauliflower, and even kale.

Salad spinner. A salad spinner is an optional juicing tool. You can spin your greens dry, but I quite like feeding my juicer with greens that are still a little wet; it adds more volume and hydration to the juice.

Mixing bowls. After I prep (wash, peel, chop, and slice) my juice ingredients, I toss all the prepped items into a large mixing bowl. I save the excess parts such as peels for composting in our garden. Having all my ingredients prepped and ready in a bowl before I start juicing makes the process easier and faster. Bonus tip: I discovered that when I fill my large mixing bowl, it yields two full glasses of juice (one for me and one for my husband).

Mason jars. These popular containers have multiple uses, not least of which is that they make great, homey glasses for your fresh-pressed juice! I also use Mason jars to store herbs; I pour in a little water, enough to cover the base of the herb stems, and refrigerate the herbs in the jar like a bouquet of flowers. When stored in the refrigerator, the water in the jar helps prevent the herbs from drying out. The bouquet is a nice little surprise to welcome you each time you open the refrigerator door, and, of course, to remind you to drink your juice!

Juicing Basics

Armed with the knowledge in this section, you will be an informed shopper and educated juicer. If necessary, you can always return to this section later to refresh your memory on the tips for creating the best juice possible.

Washing and Preparing Produce

Sure, buying organic produce is a great way to avoid ingesting chemicals such as pesticides, herbicides, or synthetic fertilizers. However, it's still really important to wash all fruits and vegetables before juicing. Even organic produce contains natural microbes and bacteria on the surface. I'm sorry for this visual, but just think how many people may have handled that bunch of kale before you put it in your cart!

To streamline the process, you can do a little prep as soon as you get home from the store, such as removing the excess parts that you don't plan to juice, like radish or carrot greens, and brushing off any obvious dirt. To prevent premature wilting, save the actual rinsing of the produce until right before you juice. Also, even if you wash produce and then store it in the refrigerator, bacteria can still grow. Use a good, clean scrub brush on any produce tough enough to handle it. For softer produce, toss it in a large bowl of clean water and use your fingers to get water into all the nooks and crannies—this technique works well on foods such as kale, romaine, and blueberries. Empty the produce into a strainer, and run some more water over it. You can also add about 1 cup of vinegar to every 3 cups of water in your rinse bowl, which may help kill bacteria.

How to Use Your Juicer

Different styles of juicers operate in slightly different ways, but from a user's standpoint, the concept is generally the same. Clean and chop your ingredients to a size that easily fits down your juicer's feeder. One tip I often tell people is not to rush or overload the juicer; let the machine do the work. This is especially true with masticating juicers, which are the slowest. By all means, help your ingredients down the feeder tube with the included tamper/pusher (don't ever use your fingers!), but be careful not to overload the feeder chute or force down any stuck pieces.

I find it best to rotate the order when feeding ingredients into the juicer. For example, to make a simple juice you might add the ingredients in this order: apple, greens, ginger, lemon, apple, greens, ginger, lemon, apple, and finally the last of your greens. I like mixing it up for two reasons. First, the juice comes out mixed so I don't need to stir it as much; and second, if the juicer gets clogged with one ingredient, the next ingredient usually helps get things running smoothly again.

Finally, to maximize its longevity, it's best for the machine if you clean it right away. I usually pop the freshly pressed juice into the freezer for a few minutes to chill, giving me the opportunity to thoroughly clean my juicer so it's ready to go the next time.

DIRTY DOZEN AND CLEAN FIFTEEN

The Dirty Dozen lists fruits and vegetables most likely to be contaminated by pesticide residues. If you can, choose organic to avoid the contaminants. The Clean Fifteen is a list of fruits and vegetables least likely to be contaminated. These items can be purchased conventionally grown, rather than organically, which can keep costs down.

THE DIRTY DOZEN

1. Strawberries
2. Apples
3. Nectarines
4. Peaches
5. Celery
6. Grapes
7. Cherries
8. Spinach
9. Tomatoes
10. Bell peppers
11. Cherry tomatoes
12. Cucumbers
    + Kale/collard greens*
    + Hot peppers*

THE CLEAN FIFTEEN

1. Avocados
2. Corn
3. Pineapples
4. Cabbage
5. Sweet peas
6. Onions
7. Asparagus
8. Mangos
9. Papayas
10. Kiwi
11. Eggplant
12. Honeydew
13. Grapefruit
14. Cantaloupe
15. Cauliflower

*The Dirty Dozen list contains two additional items—kale/collard greens and hot peppers—because they tend to contain trace levels of highly hazardous pesticides.

Buying Produce

Just like most recipes, juice benefits from fresh, high-quality ingredients, which boost flavor and nutritional content. If possible, shop at a local farmers' market where produce is fresh and has traveled a short distance from farm to market! Also, get to know the people who work at your local grocery store's produce section—they're a terrific resource for getting the inside scoop on what's in season, what's new and fresh, or what has arrived that day.

How to Pick 'Em

Seasonal produce is usually the most-nutritious and least-expensive option because there is currently an abundance being harvested. No matter the variety, look for produce that is heavy for its size, vibrant in color, and free of insect damage. Make sure the outer area is neither shriveled, wrinkled, nor bruised.

When to Buy Organic

If your budget has room for organic all the time, that's great! But for most of us, it is smart to pick and choose exactly which produce we buy organic. Some produce items are more susceptible to chemicals than others. For example, organic strawberries are considered well worth the investment, because all the little nooks and crannies trap chemicals used in conventional farming, and strawberries can be difficult to wash. Conversely, some produce, like bananas, have a tough, protective outer skin that you do not eat, making them a safer nonorganic choice. Learn more about which produce is worth your organic dollar by checking out the Environmental Working Group's Dirty Dozen and Clean Fifteen lists on the opposite page.

Making Produce Last Longer

In an ideal world, we would have time each day to shop for fresh produce. However, in reality, we are busy and may only get to the grocery store once a week, so we need to make our produce last. A well-organized and clean refrigerator can actually help your produce last longer. Herbs are best stored upright in glass jars filled with water, like a bouquet of flowers; this prevents them from wilting or drying out. Fruits and vegetables are best stored in separate refrigerator drawers. As fruit ripens, it produces ethylene, which can expedite the ripening process of other produce. It only takes one bad piece of produce to ruin an entire bunch! To avoid this, keep vegetables and fruit in their own produce drawers, and don't overcrowd—they'll last longer when not packed together.

Juicing Superstars

Juicing is a great way to add new fruits and vegetables to your diet, and by "new," I definitely encourage you to expand your horizons and include foods you've never tried before. To maximize the nutritional profile of each glass of juice, I recommend including a variety of greens, fruits, and healthy boosts. Read on to learn about some of the brightest stars in the produce world, and what to do with them.

Best Greens

ARUGULA

NUTRITION: This spicy green contains vitamins C, K, and A, plus folate, calcium, iron, and copper.

HOW TO SELECT: Choose arugula that is a vibrant green with firm, dry leaves. Avoid greens that have holes or brown or yellow spots, are mushy, or smell bad.

HOW TO STORE: Store unwashed arugula in an airtight container in the refrigerator and consume within 2 to 3 days.

HOW TO PREPARE: Wash to remove dirt or bugs. Roll a bundle of arugula leaves to feed through the juicer.

BEET GREENS

NUTRITION: Don't throw away the greens on your beets! Beet greens are packed with nutrition and are wonderful for juicing. These greens contain zinc, phosphorus, vitamins K, A, and C, as well as fiber.

HOW TO SELECT: Look for colorful beet greens without any holes or wilting.

HOW TO STORE: Thoroughly wash, and store greens between paper towels in a plastic bag or airtight container in the refrigerator's crisper drawer. Enjoy within 2 to 3 days.

HOW TO PREPARE: Re-wash, then roll or bunch beet greens to feed through the juicer. For salads, roughly chop.

BOK CHOY

NUTRITION: Bok choy is a cruciferous vegetable with anticancer and chemopreventive phytochemicals. This leafy green is rich in calcium and potassium, two essential nutrients for healthy blood-pressure levels and heart health. Bok choy also contains the antioxidant vitamin C, which supports the immune system while beautifying your skin and hair.

HOW TO SELECT: Bok choy, commonly referred to as Chinese cabbage, is available year-round. Look for firm, white stems with crisp, green leaves.

HOW TO STORE: Store in the refrigerator's crisper drawer and enjoy within 3 to 4 days.

HOW TO PREPARE: Remove each leaf and wash thoroughly. Fold or roll bok choy to feed through the juicer.

CABBAGE

NUTRITION: Cabbage is an overlooked wonder green! It contains nutrients such as vitamin K and anthocyanins that support cognitive function. Cabbage also contains sulfur, known as the "beautifying mineral," because it can help clear up oily and acne-prone skin.

HOW TO SELECT: Cabbage should be crisp, firm, and heavy. Avoid cabbage leaves that are fading in color.

Cabbage's peak season is November through April.

HOW TO STORE: Cabbage can be refrigerated in the crisper drawer for a month. Green and red cabbage may last even longer, up to 6 weeks.

HOW TO PREPARE: Peel off leaves and rinse them well. Fold or roll cabbage leaves to feed through the juicer.

CHARD

NUTRITION: Chard is part of the cruciferous family and is known to help in cancer prevention. It contains lutein, a naturally occurring pigment that supports eye health. Chard, also called Swiss chard, is packed with vitamins K, A, and C, plus iron, calcium, magnesium, manganese, and potassium. HOW TO SELECT: Chard varieties include rainbow chard, ruby chard, and rhubarb chard. Look for deep-green leaves with a firm stem. Chard is in season from late summer to early fall. HOW TO STORE: Wrap chard in a damp towel and store in the refrigerator's crisper drawer; enjoy within 2 to 3 days. Smaller leaves may wilt more quickly. HOW TO PREPARE: You can juice both the stem and leaf. Larger chard leaves can be cut in half first, if necessary.

COLLARD GREENS

NUTRITION: This green contains vitamins C, K, and A, plus folate, calcium, iron, copper, and soluble fiber. HOW TO SELECT: Look for collard greens with large, dark, vibrant-green leaves and no holes. HOW TO STORE: Store refrigerated in an airtight container and enjoy within 4 to 6 days. HOW TO PREPARE: Wash each collard green leaf individually, making sure to thoroughly cleanse the stem, where dirt may collect. Roll or fold to feed through the juicer.

DANDELION GREENS

NUTRITION: A saying in Ayurvedic and Chinese medicines is "bitter is better." Bitter foods such as dandelion greens support healthy digestion and detoxification, and contain calcium and iron as well as antioxidants and minerals. A cup of raw dandelion greens has 10 percent of your daily value of calcium. HOW TO SELECT: Leaves should be vibrant, crisp, and without holes or bug bites. Dandelion greens are available year-round. HOW TO STORE: Store unwashed greens can be stored in an airtight container in the refrigerator and enjoy within 4 to 5 days. HOW TO PREPARE: Wash thoroughly to remove dirt or bugs. Bundle the greens in batches to feed through the juicer.

KALE

NUTRITION: This sturdy green has anti-inflammatory and antioxidant properties that can support heart health. Kale contains vitamin C and glucosinolates, which may help detoxify the body and aid in cancer prevention. Kale also contains vitamins K, A, and B$_6$, plus copper, calcium, potassium, and iron.

HOW TO SELECT: The most common varieties usually available include lacinato kale (also known as dinosaur kale, Tuscan kale, and cavolo nero), curly kale, and ornamental kale. Look for kale with a rich, green color and firm edges that have not wilted or been infested by bugs.

HOW TO STORE: Because of kale's hardy nature, it can be stored washed or unwashed in the refrigerator. If washed, dry the kale thoroughly and store it between layers of paper towels in a container in the refrigerator's crisper drawer. Enjoy within 1 week.

HOW TO PREPARE: For most recipes, you'll want to zip the kale leaves off the stem and enjoy just the leaves. For juicing, however, you can consume the entire leaf and stem. Roll or bunch kale to feed through the juicer.

ROMAINE LETTUCE

NUTRITION: Romaine lettuce is a juicing must-have. It's one of the tastiest greens, and its water-density helps increase juice yield. Romaine also packs nutrients such as folate, vitamin K, and vitamin C, plus it's a good source of fiber.

HOW TO SELECT: Look for crisp romaine leaves without holes or brown spots.

HOW TO STORE: Washed and dried romaine can be stored in an airtight container in the refrigerator for 5 to 6 days.

HOW TO PREPARE: If the romaine leaves are still attached to the root, chop off the root and thoroughly wash each leaf before eating or juicing. Roll or fold romaine to feed through the juicer.

NUTRITION: Spinach is a real super-food, but it's also a great green for juicing because of its mild flavor and rich nutrition profile. Like most dark leafy greens, spinach contains iron, calcium, potassium, and folate. Spinach is also high in zinc, an important mineral supporting immune system function.

HOW TO SELECT: Spinach can easily turn slimy. Look for crisp, dry green leaves without holes.

HOW TO STORE: Store unwashed spinach in an airtight container in the refrigerator and enjoy within 2 to 3 days.

HOW TO PREPARE: Soak leaves in water, rinse, and pat dry. Roll a bundle of spinach leaves to feed through the juicer.

Powerhouse Fruits and Veggies

APPLES

NUTRITION: Apples contain anti-oxidant compounds known as flavonoids, which may prevent and repair oxidative damage. Apples also contain pectin, a soluble fiber that can bind to cholesterol, helping lower total cholesterol levels.

HOW TO SELECT: While apples are available year-round, fall is the ideal apple season. Look for apples with a firm, colorful exterior and no holes, bruises, or soft spots.

HOW TO STORE: Apples produce ethylene, a gas that speeds up the ripening of other fruits around them. Store apples in their own bag in the refrigerator. Properly kept, apples can last in the refrigerator for 1 to 2 months.

HOW TO PREPARE: Wash, core, and slice apples before feeding through the juicer.

AVOCADO

NUTRITION: Avocados can't be juiced, but they can add creaminess and nutritional value to any blended juice or smoothie. Avocados contain heart-healthy monounsaturated fats and help the body increase the absorption of fat-soluble vitamins such as A, D, E, and K.

HOW TO SELECT: Ripe avocados are dark-green and firm but yielding to gentle pressure. The peel of an over-ripe avocado will appear dark, almost black, and have very soft or indented spots. Unripe avocados may be hard and have bright-green coloring or spots. Buy a mix of unripe and ripe avocados to have a steady pipeline of avocados ready to enjoy now and later in the week.

HOW TO STORE: Store fully ripe avocados, unpeeled, in the refrigerator. Once peeled, they oxidize quickly and turn brown.

HOW TO PREPARE: Slice the avocado in half, remove the pit, and slice into wedges before adding to blended juices or meals.

BEETS

NUTRITION: Beets contain glutathione, a compound that supports digestive and liver function. This root vegetable is also high in antioxidants and contains magnesium, potassium, copper, folate, and even a little protein.

HOW TO SELECT: Look for rich, vibrantly colored beets with firm roots and no bruising or soft spots.

HOW TO STORE: If stored properly, beets can last 2 to 3 weeks. For best results, wash and gently scrub the beets, pat dry, and store in paper towels or a plastic bag in the refrigerator.

HOW TO PREPARE: Beet greens can be dirty, so remove and wash before juicing. For juicing beets, wash and cut the rounds into an ideal size for easily feeding the juicer.

BELL PEPPERS

NUTRITION: Bell peppers contain significantly more vitamin C than an orange! They're also rich in lycopene, a carotenoid pigment and phytonutrient with antioxidant benefits. Lycopene may support heart and eye health and offer neurological benefits.

HOW TO SELECT: Look for firm, shiny, unwrinkled peppers.

HOW TO STORE: Store unwashed bell peppers in the refrigerator's crisper drawer; they should last 1 to 2 weeks. Washing before storing can cause peppers to rot or turn slimy.

HOW TO PREPARE: Wash and slice bell peppers before juicing, blending, or adding to recipes.

BLUEBERRIES

NUTRITION: Blueberries are a low-sugar fruit high in antioxidants. They also contain fiber, and have been known to boost cognitive function due to their high amounts of phenols.

HOW TO SELECT: Look for rich blue-purple blueberries. Avoid berries that have green spots; they will be unripe and tart. Also watch for blueberries that are moldy or mushy.

HOW TO STORE: Store unwashed blueberries in an airtight container in the refrigerator and enjoy within 3 to 4 days. Wait to wash berries until right before eating—cleaning them before storing can hasten mold growth.

HOW TO PREPARE: No prep needed; enjoy them as they are or toss them into your juicer!

CARROTS

NUTRITION: Carrots contain beta-carotene, a compound touted for improving eyesight, preventing memory loss, and lowering the risk of diabetes. Carrots also contain vitamins A, C, K, and B_6, plus folate and fiber.

HOW TO SELECT: Colors may vary from orange to yellow to purple—as long as they're bright and colorful. Avoid carrots that look dry or limp.

HOW TO STORE: Keep carrots stored in the refrigerator's crisper drawer. To keep carrots crisp and fresh, you can also wash and slice them, and store in a container with filtered water.

HOW TO PREPARE: Remove the green tops, wash, peel (optional), and cut into a convenient size for juicing or snacking.

CELERY

NUTRITION: Celery contains riboflavin, vitamin B$_6$, pantothenic acid, calcium, magnesium, phosphorus, and lots of dietary fiber. Celery is hydrating and packed with electrolytes.

HOW TO SELECT: Look for crisp, firm celery. Avoid celery with yellowing leaves.

HOW TO STORE: Wash and slice celery, and store it in a glass jar filled with filtered water.

HOW TO PREPARE: Celery needs very little prep. Just wash and cut the celery to feed through the juicer. You can also juice the celery leaves.

COCONUT

NUTRITION: Coconuts contains lauric acid and caprylic acid, both of which have antifungal and antibacterial properties. Coconut is a great source of medium-chain triglycerides (MCTs), which are known for maximizing heart, immune, and cognitive health, while also improving energy levels and mood.

HOW TO SELECT: Look for a coconut that feels heavy and full. Brown coconuts may have more white coconut meat, while green coconuts may contain more coconut water. Avoid brown coconuts with mold or moisture in the shell's "eyes."

HOW TO STORE: Store in the refrigerator and enjoy within 3 to 4 days.

HOW TO PREPARE: Crack the coconut open and save the coconut water to add to your juices. With a spoon, separate chunks of coconut meat for blended juices or smoothies.

CUCUMBERS

NUTRITION: Cucumbers are water-dense, hydrating vegetables that contain vitamins A and C, plus multiple B vitamins.

HOW TO SELECT: Look for firm cucumbers with no bruising or soft or slimy spots.

HOW TO STORE: Store dry cucumbers in a paper towel in the refrigerator, and enjoy within 10 days.

HOW TO PREPARE: Wash, peel (optional), and cut into the most convenient size for juicing or blending.

GRAPEFRUIT

NUTRITION: Health-supportive grapefruits contain vitamins A, C, B$_1$, and B$_5$, plus potassium, biotin, antioxidants, lycopene, and phytonutrients.

HOW TO SELECT: Look for grapefruits with firm, smooth skin free of blemishes, soft spots, or major discoloration. Grapefruits can be available year-round, although they're typically in-season during the winter months.

HOW TO STORE: Grapefruits can be stored at room temperature for 1 week, or in the refrigerator for 2 to 3 weeks.

HOW TO PREPARE: Peel and segment the grapefruit flesh for feeding through the juicer.

KIWIFRUIT

NUTRITION: The unassuming but exotic kiwifruit has four times the vitamin C of an orange and as much potassium as a banana! This treat is also high in fiber, loaded with antioxidants, and delivers great flavor as a low-sugar, low-glycemic fruit.

HOW TO SELECT: Look for plump kiwi that yields to gentle pressure. Avoid kiwi that is shriveled or blemished.

HOW TO STORE: You can store kiwi in the refrigerator for up to 2 weeks.

HOW TO PREPARE: Kiwi should be peeled, then sliced and enjoyed out of hand or juiced in your favorite recipe.

LEMONS

NUTRITION: Lemons contain a variety of nutrients including the antioxidant vitamin C, potassium, and pectin (a type of fiber that supports satiety and digestive health). Lemon juice is structurally similar to stomach digestive juices, so it aids in digestion and boosts gastrointestinal health.

HOW TO SELECT: Look for unblemished lemons that are vibrant in color, are firm but with a gentle give, with no green spots.

HOW TO STORE: Lemons stored on the counter are best enjoyed within 1 week before they begin to harden. Lemons stored in a bag in the refrigerator can last longer and better retain their juice.

HOW TO PREPARE: Remove the peel and slice the lemon into pieces to feed through the juicer. Lemons with a thin peel can be sliced into wedges, so you'll juice the entire fruit, peel and all.

ORANGES

NUTRITION: One orange provides 130 percent of your daily intake of vitamin C! They also contain vitamins A and B$_6$, plus calcium, and potassium.

HOW TO SELECT: Look for oranges that are firm with a gentle give. Avoid oranges with bruises or soft spots.

HOW TO STORE: Store oranges in the refrigerator and enjoy within 2 weeks.

HOW TO PREPARE: Peel and segment oranges before feeding through the juicer.

PINEAPPLE

NUTRITION: Pineapple contains bromelain, an enzyme known for supporting protein digestion. It also has anti-inflammatory properties, plus vitamin C, fiber, and manganese.

HOW TO SELECT: Look for pineapples that are plump and fresh-looking. A good sign of a ripe pineapple is firm skin and fresh green leaves.

HOW TO STORE: Whole pineapple can be stored on the counter at room temperature and enjoyed within 2 to 4 days.

HOW TO PREPARE: Cut off the top and bottom of the pineapple. Stand the pineapple and trim away the peel. Cut the pineapple into quarters and then into slices or chunks for juicing.

STRAWBERRIES

NUTRITION: Strawberries are a deceptively low-sugar fruit containing vitamin C, folate, potassium, magnesium, and fiber.

HOW TO SELECT: Look for firm, bright-red berries. Size and shape can vary, but do not affect nutritional profile or taste. Avoid strawberries with brown or mushy spots, and berries with white, yellow, or green spots, which indicate that they are unripe.

HOW TO STORE: Store unwashed strawberries in an airtight container in the refrigerator and enjoy within 3 to 4 days. Don't wash the berries until right before eating, or else they can quickly mold.

HOW TO PREPARE: Pick off the green stems (or leave them on if you prefer), and cut into pieces for juicing.

Healthy Boosts

PARSLEY

NUTRITION: Parsley contains a variety of antioxidants including luteolin, apigenin, lycopene, beta-carotene, and alpha-carotene. These superhero antioxidants help fight free radicals, slow the aging process, and reduce inflammation. Parsley also contains vitamins A, K, and C, plus folate, iron, potassium, calcium, and magnesium.

HOW TO SELECT: Look for parsley with bright-green leaves that are not wilted or yellowing.

HOW TO STORE: Chop off the ends of the stems, and place them upright in a glass jar with a bit of filtered water in the refrigerator. Enjoy within 2 weeks.

HOW TO PREPARE: Rinse, then fold or bunch (both leaves and stems) to feed through the juicer.

CILANTRO

NUTRITION: Cilantro has strong antioxidant properties and contains vitamins A and K as well as folate and potassium. Cilantro is known to help cleanse the body of heavy metals by binding to these metals and speeding up their excretion.

HOW TO SELECT: Look for cilantro with bright-green leaves that are not wilted or yellowing.

HOW TO STORE: Chop off the ends of the stems, and place them upright in a glass jar with a bit of filtered water in the refrigerator. Enjoy within 2 weeks.

HOW TO PREPARE: Rinse, then fold or bunch (both leaves and stems) to feed through the juicer.

CINNAMON

NUTRITION: Cinnamon is abundant in antioxidants and anti-inflammatories known to help reduce the risk of heart disease, high cholesterol, and high blood-pressure.

HOW TO SELECT: Look for sticks of cinnamon with a fragrant, sweet smell.

HOW TO STORE: Stored in an airtight container, cinnamon sticks may last up to a year.

HOW TO PREPARE: Add cinnamon sticks to a high-speed blender or food processor, and pulse for 30 seconds or until it is an evenly-ground powder.

GINGER (FRESH)

NUTRITION: Ginger is known to relieve digestive distress, nausea, motion sickness, and appetite loss, and it has anti-inflammatory properties.

HOW TO SELECT: Look for fresh ginger root with a thin skin and no mold.

HOW TO STORE: Store fresh ginger in an airtight container or bag in the refrigerator. It can also be frozen.

HOW TO PREPARE: Peel ginger, slice or roughly chop it, then feed it through your juicer or blend.

TURMERIC (FRESH)

NUTRITION: Turmeric contains curcumin, a compound known to possess anti-inflammatory benefits.

HOW TO SELECT: Look for fresh turmeric root with no signs of mold.

HOW TO STORE: Store fresh turmeric in an airtight container or bag in the refrigerator.

HOW TO PREPARE: Peel, slice, or chop, and feed your juicer, or blend.

HEMP SEEDS

NUTRITION: Hemp seeds contain valuable omega-3 and omega-6 fats as well as fiber and protein.

HOW TO SELECT: Look for organic shelled hemp seeds (aka hemp hearts).

HOW TO STORE: Store hemp seeds in an airtight container in the refrigerator or freezer, and enjoy within 1 year.

HOW TO PREPARE: Shelled hemp seeds require no prep.

FLAXSEED

NUTRITION: Flaxseeds contains heart-healthy ALA omega-3 fats, fiber, and protein. The nutrients in flaxseed support skin, hair, and digestive health. Lignans in flaxseed have been associated with benefitting menopausal women due to their estrogenic properties.

HOW TO SELECT: Seek out ground flaxseed, as it is difficult for the body to digest and absorb nutrients from whole flaxseed.

HOW TO STORE: Store flaxseed in an airtight container in a cool, dark place. If stored in the pantry, enjoy within 1 year. If refrigerated or frozen, it can last 2 years.

HOW TO PREPARE: Ground flaxseed require no prep—they are ready to enjoy! Add to juice, blended juice, or recipes.

CHIA SEEDS

NUTRITION: Chia seeds contain omega-3 fats, protein, and fiber, and they incredibly expand in liquid, helping create a feeling of fullness. Their sponge-like consistency also makes them useful for binding to dietary fats and toxins and helping excrete them from the body.

HOW TO SELECT: Look for whole chia seeds.

HOW TO STORE: Store chia seeds in an airtight container in the refrigerator or freezer, and enjoy within 1 year.

HOW TO PREPARE: Chia seeds require no prep—they are ready to enjoy! Add to juice, blended juice, or recipes.

PUMPKIN SEEDS

NUTRITION: Pumpkin seeds contain zinc, an important mineral for immune system function, as well as skin, hair, and reproductive health.

HOW TO SELECT: Choose raw, organic, unsalted seeds.

HOW TO STORE: Store pumpkin seeds in an airtight container in the refrigerator, and enjoy within 6 months.

HOW TO PREPARE: Pumpkin seeds require no prep—they are ready to enjoy! Add to juice, blended juice, or recipes.

SPIRULINA

NUTRITION: Spirulina is a blue-green algae that contains protein, iron, and chlorophyll, and is known for its antimicrobial properties in fighting candida, a yeast overgrowth. Spirulina has also been associated with lowering blood pressure, detoxifying the body of heavy metals, reducing cholesterol, and boosting energy.

HOW TO SELECT: Look for organic spirulina powder.

HOW TO STORE: Store spirulina in an airtight container in the refrigerator, and enjoy within 12 months.

HOW TO PREPARE: Ground or powdered spirulina requires no prep—it's ready to enjoy! Add to juice, blended juice, or recipes.

CHLORELLA

NUTRITION: Chlorella is a blue-green algae rich in nutrients such as phytonutrients, biotin, potassium, phosphorus, zinc, iron, magnesium, vitamin A, and B vitamins. Chlorella may help the body detoxify from heavy metals.

HOW TO SELECT: Look for organic powdered chlorella or chlorella tablets.

HOW TO STORE: Store chlorella in an airtight container in the refrigerator, and enjoy within 1 year.

HOW TO PREPARE: Ground or powdered chlorella requires no prep—it's ready to enjoy! Add to juice, blended juice, or recipes.

WHEATGRASS

NUTRITION: Wheatgrass contains the carotenoid beta-carotene, plus chlorophyll, vitamin E, and antioxidant properties. Wheatgrass works to purify the blood, reduce inflammation, and detoxify the body.

HOW TO SELECT: Look for fresh or frozen wheatgrass packets.

HOW TO STORE: Fresh wheatgrass should be juiced and consumed within a few days.

HOW TO PREPARE: Wheatgrass can be juiced and consumed as a wheatgrass shot, or added to juices or smoothies. Avoid blending wheatgrass.

CREATING YOUR OWN JUICE CONCOCTION

If you're ready to experiment with your favorite ingredients, let's first take a moment to go through the checklist of the four components of a successful juice.

BASE: Always include at least one water-dense ingredient—this is the base of your juice. Using water-dense produce as the base will yield a higher quantity of juice. Romaine lettuce, celery, cucumbers, and even broccoli stems are great juice bases. These vegetables have winning base criteria: They contain lots of juice and a mild flavor that won't overpower. You may opt for one base or a combination of water-dense produce. You can also use fruit as the base—such as citrus, pineapple, or grapes—although this will create a juice with higher sugar levels. Admittedly, that can be a really tasty treat on occasion! For everyday juicing, however, I use and recommend water-dense veggies for the base.

GREENS: Having low to no sugar, greens are packed with vitamins, minerals, antioxidants, phytonutrients, and enzymes. If juicing for health is your goal, load up on greens. Aim to include at least two or three different greens such as kale, spinach, and parsley. In fact, when juicing for health, it's best to keep your juice as green-powered as possible. Also, don't forget to rotate your greens. If you find yourself always juicing spinach or kale, switch it up and try dandelion greens or cabbage. This will infuse your diet with flavor and nutritional variety, and who knows where your next favorite green will come from? And if you notice that your juice tastes too earthy, you can add fewer greens next time, or add a piece of fruit to sweeten it up.

FRUITS: Adding fruits helps sweeten a juice so it tastes great—but there's more. Fruits also provide a plethora of vitamins and minerals for added nutritional value. Lower-sugar fruits include green apples, kiwis, and berries, while water-dense fruits such as watermelon, pineapple, strawberries, melons, kiwis, and grapes will yield the most juice.

BOOSTS: Herbs, spices, powders, and seeds are a great way to boost flavor and nutritional power. I love juicing fresh ginger root or turmeric root, or adding a pinch of cinnamon to my finished juice. Herbs are also fun boosts and can add a lot of flavor. If you add boosts such as chia seeds, hemp seeds, or flaxseed after you've juiced, make sure to give your juice a good stir or shake to mix up the ingredients. Boosts aren't just about flavor either. For example, you can also increase the volume of your juice by adding fresh coconut water. Be mindful to not overly dilute fresh juice or you could detract from the flavor and decrease nutritional value. Lastly, you can experiment with adding various powders to juice—try wheatgrass, adaptogenic herbs, or protein powder. I particularly recommend adding powders to blended juices or smoothies for an enhanced taste and texture experience.

3 The Plant-Powered Juicing Plan

Welcome to the Plant-Powered Juicing Plan! My hope is that this plan helps you fall in love with fresh juice, and that by drinking juice regularly, you will notice a big boost in your health and energy levels. I wanted to create a juice plan that's exciting and realistic, so that after familiarizing yourself with it you will think, *I can do this!* That's why in addition to fresh juice—which may feel like a stretch as a stand-alone menu choice—you'll find blended juices, simple meals, and snacks.

Pick Your Launch Date

Before you begin, look at your calendar. Life is busy, and no doubt every week is filled with tasks grabbing our attention, but if we wait until the timing is perfect, we may never get started! So, do your best to find the least busy time to begin. It may be easiest to start on a weekend when you can be home to shop, make fresh juices, and do meal prep.

Prepare Your Body

Preparation is key for success! It's best to take a week or two to wrap your head around the concept before you begin. Test out a few juices, and familiarize yourself with the process of juicing before you get going. If you just purchased a juicer, read the manual. Stock your refrigerator with plenty of produce and plant-based foods. It's also wise to take time to mentally, emotionally, and physically prepare for the dietary changes ahead. With any dietary change, you can expect to face a few challenges. You may feel tempted to quit, or you may have people question your dietary decisions. If you expect these moments, you won't be caught off guard, and you will be able to handle them with confidence. I also recommend sharing with your family and friends your thoughts about this plan, and encourage those around to join you in the pursuit of optimal health! Having a support system can make a big difference in the outcome.

It will help to begin reducing the following foods from your diet:

- Alcohol
- Caffeine
- Dairy
- Fast foods
- Foods with added sugar
- Foods made with white flour
- Processed foods
- Processed and low-quality meats

Instead of thinking about what you're leaving behind, focus on what you're adding: fresh, whole foods such as fruits, vegetables, nuts, seeds, legumes, whole grains, herbs, and spices.

You'll notice that the 5-day plan in this book is 100 percent plant-based. That's because plant-based foods provide the body with not only vital macronutrients such as protein, fat, and carbohydrates, but also vitamins, minerals, fiber, antioxidants, enzymes, and phytonutrients. With the right amount of plant-based foods, you are nutritionally "covered," and can safely reduce your intake of animal-based foods. Depending on your personal preferences, you may wish to keep eating animal-based proteins. If you choose to incorporate animal-based protein into your daily diet, aim to eat the best stuff: Wild-caught salmon and organic, free-range chicken and eggs in small to moderate amounts.

It's helpful to reduce or eliminate your intake of dairy. Dairy is a common food allergen, which may contribute to dietary distress. Dairy is also commonly listed as an acid-forming pro-inflammatory food. If you like dairy in your smoothies or tea, make a conscious effort to test out and switch to dairy-free options such as unsweetened almond milk, rice milk, or coconut milk. If you currently consume a high-dairy diet, take a few weeks to reduce your intake of dairy, while simultaneously testing out and increasing your intake of plant-based alternatives. Many people fear giving up dairy and are frankly not sure how they could possibly get by without their daily yogurt, cheese, or creamer. I know this because I was one of those people, but it was easier to give up dairy than I realized. I found new foods, and I quickly started feeling so much better without the dairy that I didn't miss it one bit. I have since seen this same scenario play out for hundreds of my clients and online followers! If you're worried about giving up dairy, just know that you're not alone. Thousands of people have stood where you are and have made it through—and even more, they're happy and feeling better because of it.

Exercise is wonderful for both physical and mental health. Because this plan is a nourishment plan, not a calorie-restrictive plan, by all means continue with your current exercise routine. However, listen to and honor your body. If you feel tired, it's okay to take time to rest. You're changing your body's fuel, and this may change your body's reaction to exercise. During the transition, gentle exercise such as walking or stretching is a great way to improve blood circulation and boost your mood, both of which can help you feel better overall!

The Plant-Powered Juicing Plan

Now that we've walked through how it works, it's time to map out a schedule for your juice plan. The times listed in the plan are just suggestions, so feel free to adjust them to work with your schedule. I recommend kicking off each day with a hot mug of water with a squeeze of fresh lemon juice within half an hour of rising, and enjoying breakfast within one to two hours of rising. After that, aim to eat every three to four hours to manage appetite and blood sugar levels. Oh yes, honor your hunger cues! If you feel hungry, add an additional snack or juice recipe from those provided in this book. And if you feel full, you do not need to clean your plate! Mindful and intuitive eating is so important for healthy eating and for maintaining a positive long-term food-body relationship, so sit and savor your food, and listen to your body. Here are some additional tips:

- **Modify to your preferences.** This plan is just an example; it can easily be changed up to meet your personal dietary needs and recipe preferences. For example, if you have a favorite blended-juice recipe from this book, feel free to swap it for one of the blended juices listed in the schedule.

- **Save your juice pulp.** Some of the snack and supper recipes include juice pulp. I've organized the plan so you will create juice pulp the day before a recipe calls for it, so don't throw it out!

- **Keep it realistic and simple.** I've included new recipes to try at each meal, every day through the plan, to provide variety. However, you may find it realistic to meal-prep 2 or 3 snacks or meals and repeat them throughout the 5 days. Enjoying leftovers is totally okay!

- **Write down your experience.** Use the journaling pages on page 52 to process your thoughts and goals for the 5-day plan. Note recipes you've tried, tips you've learned along the way, and how your body feels each day.

Shopping Lists

I've provided two shopping lists. The first will provide you with all the pantry items for the 5 days, plus produce for days 1, 2, and 3. The second list is for the produce for days 4 and 5. This is designed to avoid wilting of fresh produce, although if you prefer, you can combine the two lists and just shop once before you start the plan. Some produce may wilt, but proper storage can help preserve them (see Juicing Superstars for storage recommendations, page 26). Here's another tip: If you have a masticating or twin-gear juicer, you can also juice-prep midweek for the remaining days, which will use up your produce before it wilts.

SHOPPING LIST FOR DAYS 1, 2, and 3

Fruit
- Apples, green (7)
- Bananas (3)
- Blueberries (¼ cup)
- Grapefruit (1)
- Lemons (8)
- Limes (4)
- Orange, navel (1)
- Pineapple (1½ cups)

Vegetables
- Beet (1)
- Bell pepper, red (1)
- Bok choy (6 cups)
- Carrots (4 large)
- Carrots, baby (1 cup)
- Celery (2 stalks)
- Chard, rainbow (5 cups)
- Cilantro (¾ cup)
- Cucumbers (6)
- Dandelion greens (¾ cup)
- Garlic (2 cloves)
- Ginger root (4-inch)
- Kale (2 cups)
- Lemongrass (3 stalks)
- Lettuce, romaine (19 cups)
- Onion, red (1 small)
- Onion, white (1 small)
- Spinach (6 cups)
- Sweet potatoes (2)
- Turmeric root (1-inch)

Canned and Bottled Items

- Almond milk, unsweetened (2 cups)
- Beans, black (1 [15-ounce] can)
- Beans, pinto (1 [15-ounce] can)
- Beans, white (1 [15-ounce] can)
- Chickpeas (1 [15-ounce] can)
- Chiles, green (2 [4-ounce] cans)
- Coconut milk, full-fat (1 [13.5-ounce] can)
- Lentils (2 [15-ounce] cans)
- Salsa
- Tomatoes, crushed (1 [28-ounce] can)
- Vegetable broth (2 cups)

Other

- Milk, almond

Pantry

- Almonds, raw
- Baking powder
- Baking soda
- Brown-rice pad Thai noodles
- Burger buns
- Butter, coconut
- Cacao powder
- Cashews, raw
- Chia seeds
- Coconut, unsweetened shredded
- Dates, Medjool, pitted
- Flaxseed, ground
- Flour, almond
- Flour, brown-rice
- Flour, coconut
- Shelled hemp seeds
- Herbal tea
- Hot sauce
- Molasses
- Oats, rolled
- Oil, coconut
- Oil, olive
- Olives, black
- Pecans, raw
- Pickles
- Pumpkin seeds
- Quinoa, uncooked
- Tahini

Spices

- Black pepper
- Cayenne powder
- Chili powder
- Cinnamon, ground
- Cumin, ground
- Garlic powder
- Nutmeg, ground
- Onion powder
- Oregano
- Paprika, regular and smoked
- Pumpkin pie spice
- Sea salt
- Vanilla extract

SHOPPING LIST FOR DAYS 4 and 5

Fruit

- Apples, green (2)
- Avocados (2)
- Banana (1)
- Blueberries, fresh (1½ cups)
- Lemons (3)
- Lime (1)
- Orange, navel (1)
- Pear (1)
- Raspberries, fresh (1 cup)
- Strawberries, fresh (1½ cups)
- Tomato, large (1)
- Tomatoes, cherry (¼ cup)

Vegetables

- Carrots, large (4)
- Celery stalks (2)
- Cilantro, fresh (1 bunch)
- Cucumbers (3)
- Garlic (3 cloves)
- Ginger root (2-inch)
- Kale (2 cups)
- Lettuce, romaine (14 cups)
- Onion, white, small (1)
- Parsley, fresh (1 bunch)
- Spinach (4 cups)
- Zucchini (1)

	DAY **1**	DAY **2**
EARLY AM	Hot water with lemon	Hot water with lemon
BREAKFAST (7 A.M.)	Citrus Booster (PAGE 135)	Kale Kick-Starter (Blended Juice) (PAGE 75)
SNACK (10 A.M.)	Almond Chia Energy Bites (PAGE 186)	Pumpkin Pecan Overnight Oats (PAGE 194)
LUNCH (1 P.M.)	Creamy Greens (Blended Juice) (PAGE 93)	Rooted in Health (Blended Juice) (PAGE 150)
SNACK (4 P.M.)	Calm as a Cucumber (PAGE 109)	Beet Brain Fog (PAGE 126)
DINNER (7 P.M.)	Lemongrass Coconut Noodle Soup (PAGE 188)	Loaded Sweet Potatoes (PAGE 172)
EVENING	Herbal tea or hot water with lemon	Herbal tea or hot water with lemon

DAY 3	DAY 4	DAY 5
Hot water with lemon	Hot water with lemon	Hot water with lemon
Tropical Greens (PAGE 88)	Kitchen Garden (PAGE 102)	Good Morning Green Juice (PAGE 84)
White Bean Lemon Hummus and Carrots (PAGE 198)	Carrot Coconut Muffins (PAGE 192)	Savory Snack Bites (PAGE 188)
Creamy Carrot (Blended Juice) (PAGE 133)	Spiced Pear (Blended Juice) (PAGE 96)	Berry Avo-Blast (Blended Juice) (PAGE 116)
Green Limeade (PAGE 104)	Very Berry Juice (PAGE 108)	Lemon Chia Elixir (PAGE 88)
Chickpea Beet Burgers (PAGE 182)	Quinoa Burrito Bowl (PAGE 170)	Veggie Lentil Chili (PAGE 152)
Herbal tea or hot water with lemon	Herbal tea or hot water with lemon	Herbal tea or hot water with lemon

DAILY JOURNAL

This plan may be only five days long, but it's an adventure, and as with any adventure, journaling the experience can be informative and empowering. Take note of how you feel when you wake up in the morning, after you've eaten your meals, and before bed. This practice will help you tune in to your body, recognize the changes that are happening, and honor what your body needs by making necessary adjustments. Always consider the positive: For example, do you notice a change in your bowel movements, a boost in energy, better sleep, clearer skin, or less stress? Conversely, jot down any negative feelings or symptoms you may experience. Writing down our experiences can help remind us of all the positives and allow us to work through any negatives.

DAY

1

....

....

....

....

....

....

....

....

....

....

....

DAY
2

. . . .

. . . .

. . . .

. . . .

. . . .

. . . .

DAY
3

. . . .

. . . .

. . . .

. . . .

. . . .

. . . .

DAY
4

....

....

....

....

....

....

....

....

....

....

....

DAY
5

....

....

....

....

....

....

....

....

....

....

....

Frequently Asked Questions

How will I feel on the first day? It's common to wonder if you'll feel hungry or weak on a juice- and plant-based diet. I assure you that although it's a change, plant-based foods are packed with nutrition that will provide your body with everything it needs to thrive. This plan is thoughtfully created to be nutritious and balanced. You likely will feel lighter, more energetic, and completely nourished. If you feel a little tired, listen to your body and take time to practice self-care. Increase your water intake, rest, or do something relaxing like taking a bath. If you're feeling hungry, add more plant-based protein or healthy fats to your snacks and supper—consider avocado, nuts, seeds, or legumes. These foods digest slowly and will help you feel full for longer.

Will I have withdrawal symptoms? If your previous dietary habits included a high intake of sugar, processed foods, caffeine, and/or alcohol, the dietary shift may at first leave you feeling not your best. The length of time and severity of withdrawal symptoms can vary from person to person. However, the best way out is through—and I recommend continuing to steadily nourish your body with plant-powered juices, meals, and snacks, with a mindset that states firmly, "With time I will see an improvement in how I feel, and that's why I'm here!"

Can I go to work while on this diet? Yes, absolutely! You can continue with your usual lifestyle while following the plan. To smooth the path, I recommend prepping your meals, juices, blended juices, and snacks ahead of time as often as possible, so you can bring them with you and store in a cooler or refrigerator. A masticating or twin-gear juicer really comes in handy for those who need to juice-prep, as both types of juicers yield juice that can last (when chilled) for 48 to 72 hours.

How do I make sure I get enough fiber? Because this plan contains a combination of fresh juice, blended juice, and plant-based recipes, it is packed with fiber. In fact, one blended juice can contain 15 grams, or more, of fiber, which is about half your recommended daily intake.

What if I experience digestive distress? If you currently eat a low-fiber diet, you may notice that your bowel movements change in quality and quantity. Continue to drink water to support healthy bowel movements and maintain a happy digestive tract. Focus on gut-healthy juices to nourish and calm your gastrointestinal tract as it adapts to a higher-fiber diet. Ginger is great for easing nausea, stomach distress, and diarrhea. You can add a little fresh ginger to any of the juice recipes in this book.

Can I exercise on this plan? Definitely! Continue with your regular fitness routine as you feel up to it. A walk outside or some gentle yoga may help you feel even better.

Making Juice a Part of Your Life

When you have completed the Plant-Powered Juicing Plan, congratulate yourself on the achievement! What an extraordinary investment you made into your total health and well-being. But you may wonder what's next? How do you continue in a realistic and manageable way that moves you even closer to your health goals? Let's explore!

A Glass a Day

One of the easiest ways to continue to benefit from fresh juice is to drink at least one glass of juice a day. I consume a fresh green juice and a blended juice or smoothie each day. Typically, I enjoy my green juice as an afternoon or early-evening snack. Fresh juice is always best, but one way to make juicing everyday more realistic is to juice-prep. For that, I recommend a masticating or twin-gear juicer, which you now know helps retain the nutritional quality of juice so it can be stored in the refrigerator for up to 48 hours. This way, you only have to use the juicer a few times a week and can enjoy the prepped juice the following days.

KEEP JUICING FUN!

Any healthy habit can feel boring and repetitive over time. To keep juicing fun, I encourage you to continue trying out new recipes and new fruit and vegetable combinations. Be adventurous and explore unfamiliar fruits and veggies. Just one idea is to make juice popsicles, perfect for sharing with your family or enjoying on a warm day. Simply pour your favorite juice into ice-pop molds, freeze, and enjoy. You can also sign up for a CSA box, start a garden, or visit the farmers' market to sample and get excited about new produce (see Fresh Options, page 185). You can also get creative with different ways to repurpose the juice pulp; there are definitely some great ideas in this book, but don't stop there!

Juicing on the Go

Life gets busy, and we may not always have time to make fresh homemade juice. If you're traveling, running errands, or are simply too busy, look for juice shops that promote cold-pressed and organic juices. These new juice shops are great, especially compared with store-bought juice—you never know how long that's been sitting on the shelf! In addition, store-bought juices are often pasteurized at high temperatures, which can denature nutrients, plus these products can be high in sugar or contain added sugar.

Restarting the 5-Day Plan

If you're feeling bloated, sluggish or lacking in energy, are suffering from acne or breakouts, or need a kick-start to feel better, just restart the 5-day plan! I've included 100 recipes in this book to provide you with loads of recipe inspiration. Follow the plan again just as I've created it, or swap out the recipes for others in this book—whatever you do, always have fun!

PART TWO
The Recipes

4

Morning Kick-Starters

Citrus Squeeze

SERVES

1

PREP TIME: **10 MINUTES**   JUICE TIME: **5 MINUTES**

When you think of citrus fruits, you likely think of vitamin C. However, did you know that citrus fruits also contain calcium, potassium, vitamin B6, and folate? I love this citrus juice combo of Meyer lemons, navel oranges, and grapefruit. Meyer lemons typically have a sweeter taste and more juice than traditional lemons. Grapefruits can support a healthy weight due to their enzymic fat-burning properties. The navel orange provides a flavorful sweetness to balance out the grapefruit's tang.

1 GRAPEFRUIT,
PEELED AND SEGMENTED

1 LARGE NAVEL ORANGE,
PEELED AND SEGMENTED

1 MEYER LEMON, PEELED

Cut the lemon to a size appropriate for your juicer. Process all the ingredients in the juicer, and enjoy within 1 hour.

Variation tip: *If this juice is too tangy for you, try adding an apple for natural sweetness.*

Good Morning Green Juice

SERVES
1

PREP TIME: **10 MINUTES**   JUICE TIME: **5 MINUTES**

Good morning! A green juice is a terrific way to nourish your body with vitamins and minerals first thing in the morning. This juice contains immune-boosting vitamin C from the oranges, as well as bone-strengthening iron and calcium from the spinach. Ginger is a wonderful root that supports healthy digestion and improves blood circulation. Lastly, water-dense produce such as romaine and cucumbers help increase juice volume and hydrate the body.

2 CUPS ROMAINE LETTUCE

2 CUPS SPINACH

1 CUCUMBER

1 NAVEL ORANGE,
PEELED AND SEGMENTED

¼ CUP FRESH PARSLEY

1 (1-INCH) PIECE FRESH GINGER

Prepare all the ingredients by rinsing, scrubbing, or peeling as necessary. Cut the ingredients to a size appropriate for your juicer. Process all the ingredients in the juicer, and enjoy within 1 hour.

Serving tip: *If you have leftover juice, freeze and store it as ice cubes and toss into a smoothie, or use to chill a future juice for a boost of nutrition!*

Never Miss a Beet Juice

SERVES

1

PREP TIME: **10 MINUTES**   JUICE TIME: **5 MINUTES**

Could apples be better than coffee to kick-start your morning? After drinking this juice, you may be surprised and delighted by the boost of energy you feel. Apples contain fructose, a natural energy-boosting sugar. Green apples add a delicious tart flavor. Beets are high in vitamin C and minerals such as potassium and manganese; they also contain natural sugars that will put pep in your step so you never miss a "beet!"

5 CUPS ROMAINE LETTUCE   1 BEET

1 CUCUMBER   1 LEMON

1 GREEN APPLE, CORED

Prepare all the ingredients by rinsing, scrubbing, or peeling as necessary. Cut the ingredients to a size appropriate for your juicer. Process all the ingredients in the juicer, and enjoy within 1 hour.

Substitution tip: *Not a beet fan? Use carrots!*

Melon Morning

SERVES

1

PREP TIME: **10 MINUTES**   JUICE TIME: **5 MINUTES**

Avoid melon-choly mornings; instead, sip on this vibrant, colorful, and flavorful juice to elevate your mood and energy levels, so you can power through your day. Both cantaloupe and pineapple contain nutrients that support skin health, improve eyesight, and strengthen your immune system and lungs. Cantaloupe is rich in the antioxidant beta-carotene, which converts to vitamin A. Pineapple contains bromelain, an enzyme known for aiding digestion. All the ingredients in this juice are water-dense, so look forward to a hydrating (and tasty) treat!

5 CUPS ROMAINE LETTUCE   1 LIME

2 CUPS CANTALOUPE   ½ CUP PINEAPPLE CHUNKS

Prepare all the ingredients by rinsing, scrubbing, or peeling as necessary. Cut the ingredients to a size appropriate for your juicer. Process all the ingredients in the juicer, and enjoy within 1 hour.

Variation tip: *Any melon works great in this recipe; try honeydew or watermelon.*

Ginger Carrot Orange Juice

SERVES

1

PREP TIME: **10 MINUTES**   JUICE TIME: **5 MINUTES**

This juice is beautifully bright and full of flavor. Carrots deliver a rich orange color that's attributed to their beta-carotene levels. Being an antioxidant, beta-carotene slows aging by fighting free radicals. Carrots also contain vitamins A, C, and K, plus pantothenic acid, folate, potassium, iron, copper, and manganese. As you can imagine, the addition of orange and ginger pack even more health benefits and flavor into this juice!

5 CUPS ROMAINE LETTUCE

1 CUCUMBER

2 CARROTS

1 NAVEL ORANGE, PEELED AND SEGMENTED

1 LEMON

1 (1-INCH) PIECE FRESH GINGER

Prepare all the ingredients by rinsing, scrubbing, or peeling as necessary. Cut the ingredients to a size appropriate for your juicer. Process all the ingredients in the juicer, and enjoy within 1 hour.

Ingredient tip: *Lemon peel is loaded with calcium, potassium, and vitamin C. You can juice the entire lemon, with the peel, to benefit from this additional nutrition. Note that lemon peel is slightly bitter.*

Grapefruit Ginger Green Juice

GREEN JUICE // GUT HEALTH // VEGGIE BASED

SERVES

1

PREP TIME: **10 MINUTES**   JUICE TIME: **5 MINUTES**

This citrus-themed juice stealthily packs a variety of dark leafy greens. Kale is rich in vitamin K, antioxidants, and minerals such as calcium. The nutrients in this supergreen have been known to support brain, heart, bone, skin, and hair health. Fellow supergreen spinach is loaded with iron, vitamin A, magnesium, potassium, and even a small amount of protein. And I think every juice is better with some fresh lemon juice and ginger.

2 CUPS ROMAINE LETTUCE

2 CUPS SPINACH

2 CUPS KALE

1 CUCUMBER

1 GRAPEFRUIT,
PEELED AND SEGMENTED

1 LEMON

1 (1-INCH) PIECE FRESH GINGER

Prepare all the ingredients by rinsing, scrubbing, or peeling as necessary. Cut the ingredients to a size appropriate for your juicer. Process all the ingredients in the juicer, and enjoy within 1 hour.

Substitution tip: *Some individuals may need to avoid grapefruit for health or medication reasons. Feel free to swap grapefruit for any citrus fruit, such as navel oranges.*

Lemon Chia Elixir

SERVES

1

PREP TIME: **10 MINUTES**   JUICE TIME: **5 MINUTES**

This fun juice is packed with a lemony flavor and nutritional chia seeds. Lemons support skin health and digestion, freshen breath, and are packed with the antioxidant vitamin C. It's a wonderful fruit to incorporate into your morning routine. The chia seeds are added after the produce has been juiced—they expand in liquid to create a gel-like consistency, which is very satiating. Chia can bind to dietary toxins and fats like cholesterol, and then helps excrete them. Plus, chia seeds contain fiber, healthy omega-3 fats, and even a little protein.

5 CUPS ROMAINE LETTUCE

1 GREEN APPLE, CORED

1 LEMON

1 (1-INCH) PIECE FRESH GINGER

1 TEASPOON WHOLE CHIA SEEDS

Prepare all the ingredients by rinsing, scrubbing, or peeling as necessary. Cut the ingredients to a size appropriate for your juicer. Process all the ingredients in the juicer, and enjoy within 1 hour.

Ingredient tip: *Lemon peel is loaded with calcium, potassium, and vitamin C. You can juice the entire lemon, with the peel, to benefit from this additional nutrition. Note that lemon peel has a slightly bitter flavor profile.*

Substitution tip: *This elixir is great with any citrus; try oranges, grapefruits, or even limes.*

Serving tip: *Freeze the juice into ice cubes to give chilled juice extra nutrition, or to add flavor and nutrition to your drinking water.*

Apple Carrot Orange Juice

SERVES

1

PREP TIME: **10 MINUTES**   JUICE TIME: **5 MINUTES**

Kids and adults alike will enjoy this juice! With three nutrient-rich fruits and vegetables, this juice is great if you're feeling a little under the weather and need a hit of vitamin C to boost your immune system. The best part is, this juice will keep for a while. Depending on the type of juicer you own (see Types of Juicers, page 16), this can be a great juice to prep ahead of time and keep in the refrigerator for up to three days—sip on this one first thing in the morning.

5 CARROTS   1 GREEN APPLE, CORED

1 NAVEL ORANGE,
PEELED AND SEGMENTED

Prepare all the ingredients by rinsing, scrubbing, or peeling as necessary. Cut the ingredients to a size appropriate for your juicer. Process all the ingredients in the juicer, and enjoy.

Variation tip: *When apples are in season, try different varieties such as Fuji or Gala.*

Orange Lemonade

FRUIT BASED

SERVES

1

PREP TIME: **10 MINUTES**   JUICE TIME: **5 MINUTES**

This simple orange lemonade is made with Cara Cara oranges, a type of navel orange in season December through April. Cara Cara oranges have a similar exterior to a navel orange, yet the interior reveals a vibrant pink-orange hue. They are known for being very sweet, and therefore are a perfect fit for our orange lemonade juice. This juice also contains lemon and romaine to boost juice yield and add nutritional value.

5 CUPS ROMAINE LETTUCE   1 LEMON

2 CARA CARA ORANGES,
PEELED AND SEGMENTED

Prepare all the ingredients by rinsing, scrubbing, or peeling as necessary. Cut the ingredients to a size appropriate for your juicer. Process all the ingredients in the juicer, and enjoy within 1 hour.

Variation tip: *This juice is delicious as a slushy blended with ice!*

Citrus Sunrise
BLENDED JUICE

FRUIT BASED

SERVES

1

PREP TIME: **10 MINUTES**   BLEND TIME: **1 MINUTE**

Consider this an elevated glass of morning OJ with an abundance of fiber and vitamin C that really hits the spot. Bananas add a thick, creamy consistency as well as some fiber, and turmeric and ginger are nutritional powerhouses, rich in antioxidants. Of course it wouldn't be a Citrus Sunrise without an orange! I use a classic navel orange, but you can use any citrus you prefer.

½ CUP FILTERED WATER

1 TEASPOON CHIA SEEDS

1 (½-INCH) PIECE FRESH GINGER

1 (½-INCH) PIECE FRESH TURMERIC

1 NAVEL ORANGE, PEELED AND SEGMENTED

1 BANANA, PEELED AND FROZEN

1 LEMON

½ CUP ICE

Prepare all the ingredients by rinsing, scrubbing, or peeling as necessary. Cut the ingredients to a size appropriate for your blender. Add all the ingredients to the blender, following the general principle of liquid first, lightweight ingredients next, and heaviest items on top. Blend on high for 40 to 60 seconds, and enjoy.

Ingredient tip: *For blended drinks, you can use filtered water, fresh home-made juice, unsweetened nondairy milks, or coconut water. Filtered water avoids common contaminants found in tap water, such as heavy metals.*

Serving tip: *This blended juice can be made the night before and stored in the refrigerator or freezer. Give it a good shake or second blend before enjoying!*

Honeydew Harmony

FRUIT BASED

SERVES

1

PREP TIME: **10 MINUTES**   JUICE TIME: **5 MINUTES**

This beautiful green juice has a delicate sweet-and-tangy taste. Honeydew melons are water-dense, being about 90 percent water! Don't let that fool you into thinking that honeydew melons are void of nutrients—they contain potassium, which supports heart health and muscle function, as well as vitamins A and C. Honeydew pairs nicely with two other green foods: kiwi, which is packed with vitamin C; and celery, another nutrient- and water-dense vegetable. Romaine is included for a generous boost of hydration.

5 CUPS ROMAINE LETTUCE   1 LEMON

2 CUPS HONEYDEW MELON   1 KIWI

2 CELERY STALKS

Prepare all the ingredients by rinsing, scrubbing, or peeling as necessary. Cut the ingredients to a size appropriate for your juicer. Process all the ingredients in the juicer, and enjoy within 1 hour.

Substitution tip: *Not a fan of celery? Feel free to leave it out and increase the amount of kiwi or romaine lettuce.*

Kale Kick-Starter

BLENDED JUICE

GUT HEALTH // LOW SUGAR // VEGGIE BASED

SERVES

1

PREP TIME: **10 MINUTES**   BLEND TIME: **1 MINUTE**

Kick-start your morning with this satisfying, health-supportive blended juice. Dark, leafy green kale and rainbow chard pack in the goodness of calcium and iron. A green apple adds natural sweetness plus soluble fiber, which keeps you full while reducing cholesterol levels. Chia seeds add a bit of protein as well as omega-3 fats, which support brain and heart health.

½ CUP FILTERED WATER

1 TEASPOON CHIA SEEDS

1 CUP KALE

1 CUP RAINBOW CHARD

1 (1-INCH) PIECE FRESH GINGER

1 GREEN APPLE, CORED

½ LEMON

½ CUP ICE

Prepare all the ingredients by rinsing, scrubbing, or peeling as necessary. Cut the ingredients to a size appropriate for your blender. Add all the ingredients to the blender, following the general principle of liquid first, lightweight ingredients next, and heaviest items on top. Blend on high for 40 to 60 seconds, and enjoy within 1 hour, or refrigerate or freeze overnight.

Timesaving tip: *Speed up juicing time by prepping the ingredients in advance and storing in individual bags or containers until ready to make.*

Wake Me Up

BLENDED JUICE

FRUIT BASED

SERVES

1

PREP TIME: **10 MINUTES**   BLEND TIME: **1 MINUTE**

Pear and strawberries make a perfect flavor pair! Strawberries are high in vitamin C and contain folate, potassium, manganese, dietary fiber, and magnesium. Pears provide natural sweetness, fiber, anti-oxidants, vitamins, and minerals. And creamy avocados offer healthy omega-3 fats, are cholesterol-free, and are naturally low in sodium and sugar.

½ CUP FILTERED WATER	1 PEAR, CORED
1 TABLESPOON GROUND FLAXSEED	1 CUP STRAWBERRIES
1 CUP SPINACH	1 LEMON
¼ AVOCADO, PEELED	½ CUP ICE

Prepare all the ingredients by rinsing, scrubbing, or peeling as necessary. Cut the ingredients to a size appropriate for your blender. Add all the ingredients to the blender, following the general principle of liquid first, lightweight ingredients next, and heaviest items on top. Blend on high for 40 to 60 seconds, and enjoy.

Serving tip: *Blended drinks can be made the night before and stored in the refrigerator or freezer. Just give your beverage a good shake or blend again before enjoying!*

Substitution tip: *If you're not a big fan of avocado, frozen peaches and frozen zucchini also add a creamy consistency.*

Rise, Shine, and Sip
BLENDED JUICE

SERVES

1

PREP TIME: **10 MINUTES**   BLEND TIME: **1 MINUTE**

This blended juice is so tasty and colorful, you'll look forward to waking up! Nuts and seeds provide a dose of fiber, healthy fats, and protein. Hemp seeds contain protein, omega-3s and 6s, and fiber; and chia seeds also contain omega-3 fats. Blood oranges offer vitamin C, and anthocyanins (giving citrus fruits their rich color along with antioxidants that fight free radicals and slow aging).

½ CUP FILTERED WATER

1 TEASPOON CHIA SEEDS

1 TEASPOON SHELLED HEMP SEEDS

1 CUP ROMAINE LETTUCE

1 CUP SPINACH

1 (1-INCH) PIECE FRESH GINGER

2 BLOOD ORANGES, PEELED AND SEGMENTED

½ CUP ICE

Prepare all the ingredients by rinsing, scrubbing, or peeling as necessary. Cut the ingredients to a size appropriate for your blender. Add all the ingredients to the blender, following the general principle of liquid first, lightweight ingredients next, and heaviest items on top. Blend on high for 40 to 60 seconds, and enjoy.

Ingredient tip: *No fresh ginger? Use ⅛ teaspoon of ground ginger instead.*

Serving tip: *Blended drinks can be made the night before and stored in the refrigerator or freezer. Just give your beverage a good shake or blend again before enjoying!*

Berry Grapefruit

BLENDED JUICE

FRUIT BASED

SERVES

1

PREP TIME: **10 MINUTES**   BLEND TIME: **1 MINUTE**

This beverage is full of nutrition and fiber to keep you feeling full throughout the day. Berries are a nutrient-dense, fibrous, low-sugar fruit and a good source of antioxidants such as anthocyanins, which give berries their vibrant color and anti-aging powers. You'll also benefit from the grapefruit's vitamin C content and tangy flavor, plus you'll enjoy the creamy consistency and potassium from the frozen banana.

½ CUP FILTERED WATER

½ CUP BLUEBERRIES

½ CUP STRAWBERRIES

1 GRAPEFRUIT, PEELED AND SEGMENTED

½ BANANA, PEELED AND FROZEN

½ CUP ICE

Prepare all the ingredients by rinsing, scrubbing, or peeling as necessary. Cut the ingredients to a size appropriate for your blender. Add all the ingredients to the blender, following the general principle of liquid first, lightweight ingredients next, and heaviest items on top. Blend on high for 40 to 60 seconds, and enjoy within 1 hour.

Substitution tip: *For those who can't enjoy grapefruit for health or medication reasons, use a navel orange instead. And when in season, blackberries, marionberries, or raspberries are other fun berry add-ins!*

CONVENIENT SWAPS— GREENS & VEGGIES

As you become a regular juicer, you're bound to want to experiment and come up with your own recipes and ingredient combinations—and I very much encourage this practice! Many greens and vegetables can be swapped. Learning about convenient swaps will make it easier to juice when certain greens are not available or you just want to change up the routine.

- Arugula: bok choy, cabbage, collard greens, dandelion greens, kale, spinach
- Basil: mint
- Broccoli: cabbage, cauliflower
- Cabbage: bok choy, Brussels sprouts
- Carrots: radish, sweet potato
- Celery: cucumber, radish, romaine lettuce, Swiss chard
- Cilantro: parsley
- Cucumber: celery, zucchini
- Dandelion greens: arugula, collard greens, kale, spinach, Swiss chard
- Kale: arugula, dandelion greens, spinach, Swiss chard
- Parsley: cilantro
- Radish: carrots, celery
- Romaine: butter lettuce
- Swiss chard: arugula, kale, romaine lettuce, spinach

5

All-Day Essentials

Just Peachy

SERVES

1

This sweet peachy juice has a little kick, thanks to lemon and ginger. Peaches contain vitamins E, C, and K, plus good doses of potassium and magnesium. Water-dense cucumbers are a great staple for hydrating juice recipes; in fact, a cucumber is 96 percent water! Even so, they still pack a good amount of nutrition such as vitamins A, B, and C, as well as minerals like potassium and magnesium.

5 CUPS ROMAINE LETTUCE

2 PEACHES, PEELED AND PITTED

1 CUCUMBER, UNPEELED

1 LEMON

1 (1-INCH) PIECE FRESH GINGER

Prepare all the ingredients by rinsing, scrubbing, or peeling as necessary. Cut the ingredients to a size appropriate for your juicer. Process all the ingredients in the juicer, and enjoy within 1 hour.

Ingredient tip: *Most of the nutrition is in the cucumber peel, so keep the peel on when juicing.*

Serving tip: *Juices taste best chilled! Pour this juice over ice, or pop it in the freezer for 5 minutes before enjoying.*

Sweet and Spicy

GUT HEALTH

SERVES

1

PREP TIME: **10 MINUTES**   JUICE TIME: **5 MINUTES**

If you love sweet and spicy flavors, you'll relish this juice's exotic ingredient combination! Rainbow chard, romaine lettuce, green apple, and pineapple provide a hydrating base, as well as a variety of vitamins, minerals, antioxidants, and phytonutrients. The pineapple and green apple are key players, adding a touch of natural sweetness, while a pinch of cayenne delivers heat and spice. Cayenne pepper is thought to help improve digestion, support weight loss, and support detoxification due to its ability to stimulate circulation and boost metabolism.

3 CUPS RAINBOW CHARD

3 CUPS ROMAINE LETTUCE

1 GREEN APPLE, CORED

½ CUP PINEAPPLE

1 (1-INCH) PIECE FRESH GINGER

PINCH CAYENNE PEPPER

Prepare all the ingredients by rinsing, scrubbing, or peeling as necessary. Cut the ingredients to a size appropriate for your juicer. Process all the ingredients in the juicer, and enjoy.

Timesaving tip: *Depending on the type of juicer you own, you may be able to make a double batch of this juice and refrigerate the second serving to enjoy within 72 hours (see Types of Juicers, page 16).*

Papaya Ginger

GUT HEALTH // VEGGIE BASED

SERVES

1

PREP TIME: **10 MINUTES**   JUICE TIME: **5 MINUTES**

Bok choy is an incredibly nutritious cruciferous vegetable that contains glucosinolates, whose slightly bitter flavor is thought to have cancer-fighting properties. Bok choy pairs great with sweet, juicy papaya. Papaya contains an enzyme known as papain, which has anti-inflammatory properties and helps digest proteins. Papayas are also rich in B vitamins as well as vitamins A and C.

5 CUPS BOK CHOY

1 PAPAYA, PEELED AND SEEDED

1 CUCUMBER

1 (1-INCH) PIECE FRESH GINGER

Prepare all the ingredients by rinsing, scrubbing, or peeling as necessary. Cut the ingredients to a size appropriate for your juicer. Process all the ingredients in the juicer, and enjoy within 1 hour.

Substitution tip: *You can swap bok choy for any leafy green such as romaine, kale, or spinach.*

Beet, Carrot, Ginger, and Turmeric

GUT HEALTH // VEGGIE BASED

SERVES

1

PREP TIME: **10 MINUTES**   JUICE TIME: **5 MINUTES**

This gorgeous juice has a mesmerizing purple-pink-orange color and a delicious, bold flavor. Beets contain glutathione, a compound supporting digestive and liver function. Beets are also high in anti-oxidants and contain magnesium, potassium, copper, folate, and even a little protein. They have a prominent flavor that pairs nicely with naturally-sweet produce such as the green apples and carrots in this drink.

5 CUPS ROMAINE LETTUCE

1 GREEN APPLE, CORED

1 BEET

2 CARROTS

1 (½-INCH) PIECE FRESH GINGER

1 (½-INCH) PIECE FRESH TURMERIC

Prepare all the ingredients by rinsing, scrubbing, or peeling as necessary. Cut the ingredients to a size appropriate for your juicer. Process all the ingredients in the juicer, and enjoy within 1 hour.

Ingredient tip: *If you can't find fresh ginger or turmeric, add ⅛ teaspoon each of ground, and mix well with your juice. Ground ginger and turmeric will result in a juice with more texture and grit.*

It Takes Two to Mango

SERVES

1

PREP TIME: **10 MINUTES**   JUICE TIME: **5 MINUTES**

Mango is a delectable sweet fruit! One cup of mango has 100 percent of your recommended daily intake of vitamin C, plus enough vitamin A to improve eye, bone, and skin health. It's a delicious choice to partner with rainbow chard, a colorful, nutrient-dense green. Rainbow chard contains different forms of polyphenols and carotenoid antioxidants, which fight free radicals and thus slow the aging process. In addition to its powerful antioxidant properties, rainbow chard packs an abundance of vitamins and minerals such as magnesium, potassium, calcium, copper, and vitamins C, A, and K.

5 CUPS RAINBOW CHARD

1 CUCUMBER

1 MANGO, PEELED AND PITTED

1 GREEN APPLE, CORED

1 (1-INCH) PIECE FRESH GINGER

Prepare all the ingredients by rinsing, scrubbing, or peeling as necessary. Cut the ingredients to a size appropriate for your juicer. Process all the ingredients in the juicer, and enjoy.

Serving tip: *Hooray—this is a great make-ahead juice! Store in an airtight container in the refrigerator or freezer and enjoy, ideally within 24 hours.*

Cucumber Pear

GREEN JUICE // GUT HEALTH // VEGGIE BASED

SERVES

1

PREP TIME: **10 MINUTES**   JUICE TIME: **5 MINUTES**

If you're craving a sweet green juice whose mild flavor even your kids will buy into, this is it! And like with any juice, feel free to adjust or adapt the recipe to better appeal to you or your kids' flavor preferences. For example, swap out cabbage for spinach. Parsley is a valuable herb to add to juices because it contains vital antioxidants such as luteolin, apigenin, lycopene, beta-carotene, and alpha-carotene. Parsley also contains vitamins A, K, and C, plus folate, iron, potassium, calcium, and magnesium.

5 CUPS ROMAINE LETTUCE   1 PEAR, CORED

2 CUPS CABBAGE   ¼ CUP FRESH PARSLEY

1 CUCUMBER

Prepare all the ingredients by rinsing, scrubbing, or peeling as necessary. Cut the ingredients to a size appropriate for your juicer. Process all the ingredients in the juicer, and enjoy within 1 hour.

Substitution tip: *I prefer green or Napa cabbage in this recipe. However, feel free to experiment with red cabbage, savoy cabbage, or bok choy.*

Tropical Greens

GREEN JUICE // VEGGIE BASED

SERVES

1

PREP TIME: **10 MINUTES**   JUICE TIME: **5 MINUTES**

Do you want to consume more greens, but cannot stomach the taste? Then you'll love this tropical greens juice! Green apple and pineapple add just enough natural sweetness to mask the taste of the rainbow chard and dandelion greens. Dandelion greens do taste slightly more bitter than arugula, but they contain twice as much iron as spinach—and they're also a diuretic, which means they increase urine production, naturally aiding detoxification.

2 CUPS RAINBOW CHARD

2 CUPS ROMAINE LETTUCE

1 CUCUMBER

1 GREEN APPLE, CORED

1 CUP PINEAPPLE CHUNKS

¼ CUP DANDELION GREENS

¼ CUP FRESH CILANTRO

1 (1-INCH) PIECE FRESH GINGER

Prepare all the ingredients by rinsing, scrubbing, or peeling as necessary. Cut the ingredients to a size appropriate for your juicer. Process all the ingredients in the juicer, and enjoy within 1 hour.

Ingredient tip: *If your pulp is still damp, you can re-juice the pulp to maximize yield and nutrition.*

Broccoli Pineapple Cucumber Juice

SERVES

1

What do you do with leftover broccoli stems? You juice them! For this recipe, you can juice just the stems, or go all the way and juice both the stems and the florets. Broccoli is one of the healthiest vegetables on the planet. For every bite or sip you consume, you're getting an incredible amount and variety of nutrients. To offset the broccoli flavor, pineapple, cucumber, and romaine are added to sweeten things up.

3 CUPS ROMAINE LETTUCE

2 CUPS BROCCOLI
(STEM AND FLORETS)

2 CUCUMBERS

1 CUP PINEAPPLE

Prepare all the ingredients by rinsing, scrubbing, or peeling as necessary. Cut the ingredients to a size appropriate for your juicer. Process all the ingredients in the juicer, and enjoy within 1 hour.

Variation tip: *New to juicing? It can take a little time to acclimate to the tastes of green juices. Add an apple to mask the broccoli taste even more!*

Let It Glow Juice

SERVES

1

PREP TIME: **10 MINUTES**   JUICE TIME: **5 MINUTES**

Having a rough day? Unwind and reenergize with a chilled glass of this invigorating cold-pressed juice. Inhale, exhale, sip, and repeat. This juice includes some fun-flavored ingredients such as pineapple and bell pepper. Using bell peppers in a juice may at first seem odd, yet the vegetable is sweeter than we often think, and is an excellent source of vitamins A, C, and B6.

5 CUPS ROMAINE LETTUCE

1 NAVEL ORANGE, PEELED AND SEGMENTED

1 YELLOW BELL PEPPER, CORED

½ CUP PINEAPPLE

1 (1-INCH) PIECE FRESH GINGER

1 (1-INCH) PIECE FRESH TURMERIC

Prepare all the ingredients by rinsing, scrubbing, or peeling as necessary. Cut the ingredients to a size appropriate for your juicer. Process all the ingredients in the juicer, and enjoy within 1 hour.

Ingredient tip: *Stick to yellow or orange bell peppers for this recipe, which taste sweeter than red or green.*

Cucumber, Basil, and Lime Juice

SERVES

1

PREP TIME: **10 MINUTES**   JUICE TIME: **5 MINUTES**

Think summer salad in a glass! Basil and strawberries are a satiating flavor combination. Basil is known for its antioxidant, anti-inflammatory, and immune-boosting properties. In fact, studies have shown that the nutrients in basil act as a natural adaptogen, which, as the name suggests, is a substance thought to help the body adapt to stress by balancing out hormones. Of course, the strawberries add a touch of sweetness, as well as some vitamin C.

5 CUPS ROMAINE LETTUCE   ¼ CUP FRESH BASIL

2 CUCUMBERS   1 LIME

1 CUP STRAWBERRIES

Prepare all the ingredients by rinsing, scrubbing, or peeling as necessary. Cut the ingredients to a size appropriate for your juicer. Process all the ingredients in the juicer, and enjoy within 1 hour.

Variation tip: *Blackberries are delicious in lieu of strawberries!*

Creamy Greens

BLENDED JUICE

GREEN JUICE // GUT HEALTH // VEGGIE BASED

SERVES

1

PREP TIME: **10 MINUTES**   BLEND TIME: **1 MINUTE**

This blended green juice is so creamy, thanks to the frozen banana. The greens chosen for this drink—kale, spinach, and dandelion greens—help the body thrive. Dandelion greens have a slightly bitter taste, but support healthy digestion and detoxification. And the banana and green apple do a great job of offsetting the bitter taste.

½ CUP FILTERED WATER

1 CUP SPINACH

½ CUP DANDELION GREENS

1 CUP KALE

1 BANANA, PEELED AND FROZEN

1 GREEN APPLE, CORED

½ CUP ICE

Prepare all the ingredients by rinsing, scrubbing, or peeling as necessary. Cut the ingredients to a size appropriate for your blender. Add all the ingredients to the blender, following the general principle of liquid first, lightweight ingredients next, and heaviest items on top. Blend on high for 40 to 60 seconds, and enjoy within 1 hour, or refrigerate or freeze overnight.

Ingredient tip: *For blended drinks, you can use filtered water, fresh home-made juice, unsweetened nondairy milks, or coconut water. Filtered water avoids common contaminants found in tap water, such as heavy metals.*

Timesaving tip: *Save time by prepping your ingredients ahead and storing in the freezer in small bags or containers.*

Apple Avocado

BLENDED JUICE

SERVES
1

PREP TIME: **10 MINUTES**   BLEND TIME: **1 MINUTE**

Sweet, creamy, and energizing is what this blended juice is all about! Avocado can't be juiced, but it can be added to a blended juice to provide a creamy texture as well as fiber, healthy fats, and a bit of protein. Add cilantro to almost any green drink to boost the flavor and nutrition profile. Cilantro has strong antioxidant properties and contains vitamins A and K as well as folate and potassium. If you don't like the taste of cilantro, swap it for parsley, basil, or another dark leafy green such as spinach.

1 CUP FILTERED WATER

¼ CUP FRESH CILANTRO

1 CUP ROMAINE LETTUCE

¼ AVOCADO, PEELED AND PITTED

1 GREEN APPLE, CORED

½ CUP ICE

Prepare all the ingredients by rinsing, scrubbing, or peeling as necessary. Cut the ingredients to a size appropriate for your blender. Add all the ingredients to the blender, following the general principle of liquid first, lightweight ingredients next, and heaviest items on top. Blend on high for 40 to 60 seconds, and enjoy within 1 hour, or refrigerate or freeze overnight.

Ingredient tip: *Keep the skin on the apple for a boost of fiber, as well as calcium, potassium, and vitamin C.*

Cinnamon Apple

BLENDED JUICE

SERVES

1

PREP TIME: **10 MINUTES**　　　　BLEND TIME: **1 MINUTE**

This blended juice is a comforting, classic combo of cinnamon and apple. It's the perfect beverage to enjoy in the fall—or anytime, if you're a fan of this autumnal flavor combination. Hemp seeds add protein, fiber, and healthy fats, while the green apple offers fiber and vitamin C. The spices in this drink really make it special—and they don't just smell good, but also contain a variety of health benefits: Cinnamon is known to support healthy blood sugar levels, and cardamom may support digestive health.

1 CUP UNSWEETENED ALMOND MILK

¼ TEASPOON GROUND CINNAMON

¼ TEASPOON GROUND NUTMEG

¼ TEASPOON GROUND CARDAMOM

SHELLED HEMP SEEDS

1 TABLESPOON HEMP SEEDS

1 GREEN APPLE, CORED

½ CUP ICE

Prepare all the ingredients by rinsing, scrubbing, or peeling as necessary. Cut the ingredients to a size appropriate for your blender. Add all the ingredients to the blender, following the general principle of liquid first, lightweight ingredients next, and heaviest items on top. Blend on high for 40 to 60 seconds, and enjoy within 1 hour, or refrigerate or freeze overnight.

Substitution tip: *Feeling festive? Swap all the spices in this recipe for ½ teaspoon of pumpkin pie spice!*

Spiced Pear

BLENDED JUICE

FRUIT BASED

SERVES

1

PREP TIME: **10 MINUTES**   BLEND TIME: **1 MINUTE**

This spicy-pear blended drink features a memorable cayenne-pepper kick. Cayenne pepper is thought to boost metabolism and support healthy weight loss and weight maintenance. Dates add natural sweetness (and energy!) as well as calcium, magnesium, potassium, zinc, vitamin B_6, and fiber. Chia seeds are also a wonderful blended-beverage booster, with a high fiber content that supports digestive health and bowel regularity. Yes, this drink is full of good-for-you ingredients, but don't forget that it tastes great, too!

1 CUP UNSWEETENED ALMOND MILK OR FILTERED WATER

¼ TEASPOON GROUND CINNAMON

PINCH CAYENNE PEPPER

1 TEASPOON CHIA SEEDS

3 PITTED MEDJOOL DATES

1 PEAR, CORED

½ CUP ICE

Prepare all the ingredients by rinsing, scrubbing, or peeling as necessary. Cut the ingredients to a size appropriate for your blender. Add all the ingredients to the blender, following the general principle of liquid first, lightweight ingredients next, and heaviest items on top. Blend on high for 40 to 60 seconds, and enjoy within 1 hour, or refrigerate or freeze overnight.

Ingredient tip: *To avoid damaging your blender, always double-check each date to make sure it's truly pitted before adding.*

Minty Mango

BLENDED JUICE

FRUIT BASED

SERVES

1

PREP TIME: **10 MINUTES**   BLEND TIME: **1 MINUTE**

This blended juice includes a festive combination of mint and mango. Mint, a wonderful herb for digestion, is great for cleansing the palate and freshening breath. Mango is a higher-sugar fruit, and therefore is a great natural energy booster. This beverage is loaded with fiber, which can help balance blood sugar levels and keep you feeling full. It's all rounded out with coconut water, which contains natural electrolytes such as potassium, magnesium, and sodium.

1 CUP COCONUT WATER

1 TABLESPOON FRESH MINT

½ CUP KALE

1 MANGO, PEELED AND PITTED

1 BANANA, PEELED AND FROZEN

½ CUP ICE

Prepare all the ingredients by rinsing, scrubbing, or peeling as necessary. Cut the ingredients to a size appropriate for your blender. Add all the ingredients to the blender, following the general principle of liquid first, lightweight ingredients next, and heaviest items on top. Blend on high for 40 to 60 seconds, and enjoy within 1 hour, or refrigerate or freeze overnight.

Substitution tip: *Coconut water can be swapped for any liquid such as fresh juice, filtered water, or unsweetened nondairy milk.*

6

Low-Sugar Juices

Blueberry Booster

GUT HEALTH // LOW SUGAR

SERVES

1

PREP TIME: **10 MINUTES**   JUICE TIME: **5 MINUTES**

This juice is a super booster! Kiwis are a great source of antioxidant and immune-boosting vitamin C. In fact, one kiwi fruit is packed with more than the recommended daily intake of vitamin C—there's your immune boost! Blueberries are one of the highest antioxidant foods in the world, and are loaded with phenols, known to stimulate cognitive function. But it doesn't stop there. Ginger may improve blood circulation and soothe an upset stomach. Lemon and ginger support gut health. Lemon also adds still vitamin C, important for collagen production, which plays an important role in skin and gut health. Get boosting!

5 CUPS ROMAINE LETTUCE   1 CUCUMBER

2 KIWIS   1 LEMON

1 CUP BLUEBERRIES   1 (½-INCH) PIECE FRESH GINGER

Prepare all the ingredients by rinsing, scrubbing, or peeling as necessary. Cut the ingredients to a size appropriate for your juicer. Process all the ingredients in the juicer, and enjoy within 1 hour.

Serving tip: *Freeze the juice into ice cubes to give chilled juice added nutrition, or to add flavor and nutrition to your drinking water!*

Substitution tip: *This juice works great with any berry. Mix it up with strawberries, blackberries, or raspberries.*

Greens Are Great

GREEN JUICE // GUT HEALTH // LOW SUGAR

SERVES

1

PREP TIME: **10 MINUTES**   JUICE TIME: **5 MINUTES**

Green apples are my choice for juice or blended drinks. They have a crisp, tart flavor and are slightly lower in sugar than red apples. Colors aside, all apples contain pectin, a type of soluble fiber that binds to cholesterol in the digestive tract. Romaine lettuce and cucumbers are water-dense and help yield more juice. Parsley is an excellent source of vitamin K, essential in blood clotting and preventing excess bleeding. That's what I love about fruits and veggies: They continuously impress me with the amazing benefits that come from the vitamins, minerals, and antioxidants within!

5 CUPS ROMAINE LETTUCE   1 LEMON

1 CUCUMBER   ¼ CUP FRESH PARSLEY

1 GREEN APPLE, CORED   1 (1-INCH) PIECE GINGER

Prepare all the ingredients by rinsing, scrubbing, or peeling as necessary. Cut the ingredients to a size appropriate for your juicer. Process all the ingredients in the juicer, and enjoy.

Timesaving tip: *This is a great everyday low-sugar juice that, depending on the type of juicer you own, can be made ahead of time and stored in the refrigerator for up to 72 hours (see Types of Juicers, page 16).*

Kitchen Garden

LOW SUGAR // VEGGIE BASED

SERVES

1

PREP TIME: **10 MINUTES**   JUICE TIME: **5 MINUTES**

This recipe was inspired by my very own backyard kitchen garden! I have all these vegetables and herbs growing in my yard, and I love seeing how they change every day. Just like people, plants flourish with regular love and kindness! This juice is packed with veggies and is low in sugar. The flavor profile may be a little intense for new juicers, but if you love your veggies, you'll appreciate this one and the nutritional punch it packs.

2 CUPS ROMAINE LETTUCE

2 CUPS KALE

2 CARROTS, PEELED

1 ZUCCHINI

1 CUCUMBER

1 LARGE TOMATO

1 BUNCH FRESH CILANTRO

Prepare all the ingredients by rinsing, scrubbing, or peeling as necessary. Cut the ingredients to a size appropriate for your juicer. Process all the ingredients in the juicer, and enjoy within 1 hour.

Variation tip: *You can always sweeten a juice like this by adding an apple.*

Rainbow Love

SERVES

1

PREP TIME: **10 MINUTES**   JUICE TIME: **5 MINUTES**

Do you rotate your greens? If you always use spinach when you juice, try a different green such as rainbow chard to add nutritional and flavor variety to your diet. Rainbow chard is nutrient-dense; you can tell just by looking at the rich, green leaves and vibrant, colorful stems. Juice both the leaf and stem—this will maximize the benefits from vitamins A, C, and K, plus magnesium, potassium, and iron.

5 CUPS RAINBOW CHARD	1 CUCUMBER
3 CARROTS	1 LIME, PEELED
2 CELERY STALKS	½ GREEN APPLE, CORED

Prepare all the ingredients by rinsing, scrubbing, or peeling as necessary. Cut the ingredients to a size appropriate for your juicer. Process all the ingredients in the juicer, and enjoy within 1 hour.

Serving tip: This veggie-heavy juice has a complex flavor profile you can really savor, so take your time with it—use a straw! Juices are best chilled, and that is especially true with pungent juices such as this one.

Green Limeade

SERVES

1

PREP TIME: **10 MINUTES**   JUICE TIME: **5 MINUTES**

Love lemonade? This juice is a fun twist on a classic favorite. Limes, like lemons, are packed with vitamin C. Green apple adds a delicious tangy flavor as well as natural sweetness. Spinach contains iron, calcium, potassium, and folic acid, and is also high in zinc, an important mineral for immune health. And romaine, along with cucumber, provide a terrific water-dense base for any juice.

5 CUPS SPINACH

5 CUPS ROMAINE LETTUCE

2 LIMES, PEELED

1 CUCUMBER

½ GREEN APPLE, CORED

Prepare all the ingredients by rinsing, scrubbing, or peeling as necessary. Cut the ingredients to a size appropriate for your juicer. Process all the ingredients in the juicer, and enjoy.

Timesaving tip: *Make a double or triple batch of this yummy juice—it should keep for 24 to 72 hours, depending on the type of juicer you own (see Types of Juicers, page 16).*

Calm as a Cucumber

SERVES

1

PREP TIME: **10 MINUTES**   JUICE TIME: **5 MINUTES**

Did you know that signs of dehydration include feeling edgy and having difficulty making decisions? If you're experiencing these symptoms, a glass of fresh homemade juice can hit the spot and help you feel better in no time. In this recipe, hydrating cucumbers form the base; they contain multiple B vitamins, which are our energy vitamins. Apples are another hydrating and sweet add-in. The bok choy contains calcium and potassium, two nutrients essential for restoring blood-pressure levels and maintaining heart health.

3 CUPS BOK CHOY   1 LEMON

2 CUCUMBERS   ¼ CUP FRESH CILANTRO

1 GREEN APPLE, CORED

Prepare all the ingredients by rinsing, scrubbing, or peeling as necessary. Cut the ingredients to a size appropriate for your juicer. Process all the ingredients in the juicer, and enjoy within 1 hour.

Substitution tip: *Swap bok choy for any green such as arugula, kale, spinach, or romaine.*

Very Veggie

SERVES

1

PREP TIME: **10 MINUTES**   JUICE TIME: **5 MINUTES**

This juice is a great way to nourish your body with an incredible amount of nutrition—fast. It's a flavorful vegetable juice with a slightly spicy kick provided by the radishes, which are a source of folate, riboflavin, and potassium for heart and blood-pressure health. And don't be misled by the 95 percent water content in celery—this valuable veggie also contains riboflavin, vitamin B_6, pantothenic acid, calcium, magnesium, and phosphorus.

3 CUPS ROMAINE LETTUCE

2 CUPS RAINBOW CHARD

2 CELERY STALKS

2 CARROTS

1 LEMON, PEELED

1 CUP RADISHES

½ GREEN APPLE, CORED

¼ CUP FRESH CILANTRO

Prepare all the ingredients by rinsing, scrubbing, or peeling as necessary. Cut the ingredients to a size appropriate for your juicer. Process all the ingredients in the juicer, and enjoy within 1 hour.

Variation tip: *Go ahead and taste your juice as you go, making adjustments to suit your palate. If your juice is too tart or bitter, add more apple. If your juice is too sweet, add more leafy greens.*

Pepper Power

LOW SUGAR // VEGGIE BASED

SERVES

1

PREP TIME: **10 MINUTES**   JUICE TIME: **5 MINUTES**

Bell peppers overflow with vitamin C—and of all the colors, red bell peppers contain the highest amount. One red bell pepper contains about 150 percent of your recommended daily intake! Vitamin C is an incredible antioxidant that supports immune health as well as collagen production, an important protein necessary for muscle, skin, bone-tissue, and digestive health. If you're feeling a little under the weather, this Pepper Power juice will have you feeling like your best self in no time!

5 CUPS ROMAINE LETTUCE

1 CUCUMBER

1 YELLOW BELL PEPPER

1 ORANGE BELL PEPPER

1 RED BELL PEPPER

Prepare all the ingredients by rinsing, scrubbing, or peeling as necessary. Cut the ingredients to a size appropriate for your juicer. Process all the ingredients in the juicer, and enjoy within 1 hour.

Health tip: *Do you chew your juice? If so, swish the juice around in your mouth a few times with each sip to release saliva, which contains enzymes that support digestion.*

Very Berry Juice

FRUIT BASED // LOW SUGAR

SERVES

1

PREP TIME: **10 MINUTES**   JUICE TIME: **5 MINUTES**

Berries are special because they are low in sugar yet full of flavor. They're also known for their high antioxidant properties; raspberries contain a plant polyphenol known as quercetin, which has been known to help fight cancer, mitigate heart disease, and slow the aging process. Blueberries are one of the most nutrient-dense and antioxidant-rich foods in the world—and they're irresistibly yummy! Romaine, cucumber, and lemon boost the juice yield in this recipe, but they also pack in even more vitamins, minerals, and antioxidants.

5 CUPS ROMAINE LETTUCE

1 CUP BLUEBERRIES

1 CUP STRAWBERRIES

1 CUP RASPBERRIES

1 CUCUMBER

1 LEMON, PEELED

Prepare all the ingredients by rinsing, scrubbing, or peeling as necessary. Cut the ingredients to a size appropriate for your juicer. Process all the ingredients in the juicer, and enjoy within 1 hour.

Timesaving tip: *This is a great everyday juice that, depending on the type of juicer you own, can be prepped ahead of time and stored in the fridge for up to 72 hours (see Types of Juicers, page 16).*

Dandy Dandelion Greens

GREEN JUICE // LOW SUGAR // VEGGIE BASED

SERVES

1

PREP TIME: **10 MINUTES**   JUICE TIME: **5 MINUTES**

I probably don't have to say much about spinach—its superfood status is well-known and well-deserved. But once you discover the power of dandelion greens, they'll likely become a shopping staple as well. Dandelion greens contain calcium and iron, and are abundant in antioxidants and minerals. This spicy bitter green supports healthy digestion and has been known to help maintain healthy blood sugar levels as well as reduce eczema and acne. The apple and ginger provide just enough sweet and aromatic goodness to make this a delicious treat.

4 CUPS SPINACH

2 CUPS DANDELION GREENS

1 CUCUMBER

1 GREEN APPLE, CORED

1 LEMON

1 (1-INCH) PIECE FRESH GINGER

Prepare all the ingredients by rinsing, scrubbing, or peeling as necessary. Cut the ingredients to a size appropriate for your juicer. Process all the ingredients in the juicer, and enjoy within 1 hour.

Health tip: *Fresh juice is best consumed on an empty stomach. If juice gives you heartburn or stomach upset, make sure to drink it when your stomach is empty.*

Strawberry Herb

BLENDED JUICE

LOW SUGAR

SERVES

1

PREP TIME: **10 MINUTES**   BLEND TIME: **1 MINUTE**

The yummy strawberries and flavor-enhancing basil evoke vivid memories of spring and summer. It's a light, fresh, and happy drink full of nutrition. Basil in particular is a great immune booster that contains antioxidant and anti-inflammatory properties. Bring the season's best to your body with this tasty concoction!

½ CUP FILTERED WATER

3 CUPS ROMAINE LETTUCE

¼ CUP FRESH BASIL

2 CUPS STRAWBERRIES

1 CUCUMBER

1 LEMON, PEELED

½ CUP ICE

Prepare all the ingredients by rinsing, scrubbing, or peeling as necessary. Cut the ingredients to a size appropriate for your blender. Add all the ingredients to the blender, following the general principle of liquid first, lightweight ingredients next, and heaviest items on top. Blend on high for 40 to 60 seconds, and enjoy within 1 hour, or refrigerate or freeze overnight.

Ingredient tip: *When making blended drinks, you can use filtered water, fresh homemade juice, unsweetened nondairy milks, or coconut water. Filtered water avoids common contaminants found in tap water, such as heavy metals.*

Substitution tip: *Berries and herbs go great together! Mix it up by trying blackberry and mint, or peach and cilantro.*

Apple Radish

BLENDED JUICE

GUT HEALTH // LOW SUGAR

SERVES

1

PREP TIME: **10 MINUTES**   BLEND TIME: **1 MINUTE**

This beverage gets its spicy-sweet flavor from the apple and radish. Radishes are alkaline-forming, which means they can help balance the body's pH levels, which can help prevent or slow inflammation—a critical task as inflammation is a precursor to a variety of diet-related diseases. This recipe is also great for anyone looking for a flavorful, low-sugar blended juice. Blended juices made with fruits and veggies are packed with satiating fiber, useful for those monitoring their blood sugar levels.

1 CUP FILTERED WATER

3 CUPS ROMAINE LETTUCE

1 (1-INCH) PIECE FRESH GINGER

½ CUP RADISHES

½ LEMON

½ GREEN APPLE, CORED

½ CUP ICE

Prepare all the ingredients by rinsing, scrubbing, or peeling as necessary. Cut the ingredients to a size appropriate for your blender. Add all the ingredients to the blender, following the general principle of liquid first, lightweight ingredients next, and heaviest items on top. Blend on high for 40 to 60 seconds, and enjoy within 1 hour, or refrigerate or freeze overnight.

Variation tip: *Add a serving of protein and/or healthy fats to further support healthy blood sugar levels, such as chia seeds, flaxseed, hemp seeds, plant-based protein powder, avocado, or nuts (like almonds or walnuts).*

Simple Greens

BLENDED JUICE

GREEN JUICE // GUT HEALTH // LOW SUGAR

SERVES

1

PREP TIME: **10 MINUTES**   BLEND TIME: **1 MINUTE**

Greens are powerful kinds of veggies—but most of us do not consume enough greens in a day to truly let our body thrive. Thankfully, juicing or blending is an easy and effective way to get more greens into our daily routine. This simple blended green drink contains kale, arugula, and romaine for a variety of dark-leafy-green benefits. I love including frozen banana in blended beverages to add natural sweetness and a creamy texture. If you're not a fan of banana, some avocado, frozen zucchini, or frozen peaches can provide similar creaminess.

½ CUP FILTERED WATER

1 CUP KALE

1 CUP ARUGULA

1 CUP ROMAINE LETTUCE

1 (1-INCH) PIECE FRESH GINGER, PEELED

1 BANANA, PEELED AND FROZEN

½ LEMON, PEELED

½ CUP ICE

Prepare all the ingredients by rinsing, scrubbing, or peeling as necessary. Cut the ingredients to a size appropriate for your blender. Add all the ingredients to the blender, following the general principle of liquid first, lightweight ingredients next, and heaviest items on top. Blend on high for 40 to 60 seconds, and enjoy within 1 hour, or refrigerate or freeze overnight.

Substitution tip: *If you're watching your sugar intake, swap the banana for an avocado.*

Apple Broccoli

BLENDED JUICE

SERVES

1

PREP TIME: **10 MINUTES**   BLEND TIME: **1 MINUTE**

This simple blended drink has a slightly sweet and tangy taste, delivered by the apple and lemon. It also contains a serving of super healthy broccoli. Some of the many health benefits associated with regular broccoli consumption include slowed aging, better bone health, faster wound healing, detoxification, lowered blood pressure and cholesterol levels, and improved fertility. Broccoli is truly one of the healthiest vegetables we can eat!

½ CUP FILTERED WATER

2 CUPS ROMAINE LETTUCE

½ CUP BROCCOLI

½ LEMON

1 GREEN APPLE, CORED

½ CUP ICE

Prepare all the ingredients by rinsing, scrubbing, or peeling as necessary. Cut the ingredients to a size appropriate for your blender. Add all the ingredients to the blender, following the general principle of liquid first, lightweight ingredients next, and heaviest items on top. Blend on high for 40 to 60 seconds, and enjoy within 1 hour, or refrigerate or freeze overnight.

Serving tip: *If your blended juice is too icy, add in a few slices of banana for a creamier consistency.*

Berry Avo-Blast

BLENDED JUICE

FRUIT BASED // LOW SUGAR

SERVES

1

PREP TIME: **10 MINUTES**   BLEND TIME: **1 MINUTE**

Berries and avocados are a great power couple—delicious and nutrient-rich. For those watching their sugar intake and blood sugar levels, this is a wonderful blended beverage to drink on a regular basis. The avocado, blueberry, and green apple are naturally lower in sugar than some other options. This beverage is also packed with fiber, which helps slow digestion and balance blood sugar levels. Lastly, hemp seeds add a bit of protein, which further helps manage healthy blood sugar levels.

½ CUP FILTERED WATER

2 CUPS SPINACH

1 TEASPOON HEMP SEEDS

¼ AVOCADO, PEELED AND PITTED

½ CUP BLUEBERRIES

½ CUP STRAWBERRIES

½ GREEN APPLE, CORED

½ CUP ICE

Prepare all the ingredients by rinsing, scrubbing, or peeling as necessary. Cut the ingredients to a size appropriate for your blender. Add all the ingredients to the blender, following the general principle of liquid first, lightweight ingredients next, and heaviest items on top. Blend on high for 40 to 60 seconds, and enjoy.

Serving tip: Blended drinks can be made the night before and stored in the refrigerator or freezer. Just give your beverage a good shake or blend again before enjoying!

CONVENIENT SWAPS— FRUITS & BOOSTS

As with greens and vegetables, many fruits have similar characteristics and can easily be replaced for one another in a juice recipe. Use this guide for convenient fruit and boost swaps.

Fruits
- Apples: kiwis, pears
- Blueberries: blackberries, cherries, marionberries, raspberries, strawberries
- Cantaloupe: honeydew, pineapple, watermelon
- Lemon: lime
- Lime: lemon
- Orange: grapefruit, pineapple
- Pineapple: mango, orange, papaya

Boosts
- Cacao powder: carob powder
- Cinnamon: nutmeg
- Shelled hemp seeds: ground flaxseed, pumpkin seeds
- Pumpkin seeds: shelled hemp seeds, sunflower seeds

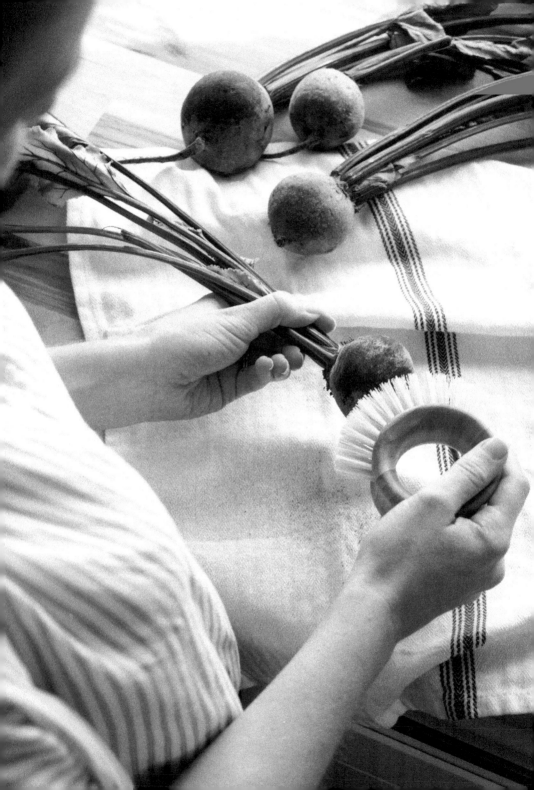

7

Brain & Energy Boosters

Green Energy Juice

SERVES

1

Energy drinks typically contain artificial ingredients, high doses of caffeine, plus added sugar (or worse, artificial sweeteners). Coffee, on the other hand, can be addictive and dehydrating. But this green juice will give you a boost of energy without any guilt or downsides! Green apples and delightful kiwi both add natural sweetness as well as vitamin C, to support a healthy, strong immune system.

5 CUPS ROMAINE LETTUCE

3 CELERY STALKS

2 GREEN APPLES, CORED

2 KIWIS

Prepare all the ingredients by rinsing, scrubbing, or peeling as necessary. Cut the ingredients to a size appropriate for your juicer. Process all the ingredients in the juicer, and enjoy within 1 hour.

Serving tip: *If you can't drink all of your juice right away, transfer it to an ice cube tray and freeze. This will allow you to use it in recipes at a later time.*

Ingredient tip: *With some produce, such as cucumbers or apples, leaving the skin on adds nutritional value. However, when it comes to produce such as kiwis or waxy fruits or vegetables, you should always peel the skin.*

Celery Sipper

GREEN JUICE // GUT HEALTH // LOW SUGAR

SERVES

1

PREP TIME: **10 MINUTES**   JUICE TIME: **5 MINUTES**

Proper hydration is vital for optimal body function—enhancing skin, tissue, and organ health while boosting your energy levels. And this juice—with ingredients such as celery, romaine, and cucumber—is the definition of hydrating. Celery also contains electrolytes, riboflavin, vitamin B_6, pantothenic acid, calcium, magnesium, and phosphorus—and if that isn't enough, it's been known to support healthy blood-pressure levels, improve liver function, and lower inflammation! Cilantro adds a flavorful kick as well as a host of nutritional benefits.

5 CUPS ROMAINE LETTUCE

5 CELERY STALKS

1 CUCUMBER

1 LEMON

¼ CUP FRESH CILANTRO

1 (1-INCH) PIECE FRESH GINGER, PEELED

Prepare all the ingredients by rinsing, scrubbing, or peeling as necessary. Cut the ingredients to a size appropriate for your juicer. Process all the ingredients in the juicer, and enjoy within 1 hour.

Substitution tip: *Not a fan of cilantro? Swap for parsley, basil, or any leafy green.*

Super Spinach Sipper

GREEN JUICE // LOW SUGAR // VEGGIE BASED

SERVES

1

PREP TIME: **10 MINUTES**   JUICE TIME: **5 MINUTES**

Superfood spinach is a nutrient-dense leafy green that is particularly rich in iron. Anemia is a form of iron deficiency resulting in weariness and fatigue. Loading up on naturally iron-rich foods such as spinach is a great way to boost energy levels and avoid anemia. Apples and cucumbers are both nutritious and hydrating to further amp up your energy. Add in a lime for tang and immune-boosting vitamin C, and you'll be on your way!

5 CUPS SPINACH   1 GREEN APPLE, CORED

2 CUCUMBERS   1 LIME

Prepare all the ingredients by rinsing, scrubbing, or peeling as necessary. Cut the ingredients to a size appropriate for your juicer. Process all the ingredients in the juicer, and enjoy within 1 hour.

Variation tip: *I love green apples for fresh juice, but you can use Gala, Fuji, or whichever variety is the apple of your eye!*

Apple Cider

LOW SUGAR

SERVES

1

PREP TIME: **10 MINUTES**   JUICE TIME: **5 MINUTES**

This juice evokes a sense of autumn with its fragrant orange, cinnamon, and apple flavors. Cinnamon is known to support healthy blood sugar levels—aka energy levels. Cinnamon also has strong antioxidant properties and is associated with better skin health, fighting allergies, and reducing the effects of aging on the brain. Romaine is a mild green that complements any juice with its added water volume and bonus serving of nutrients.

5 CUPS ROMAINE LETTUCE

1 APPLE, CORED

½ NAVEL ORANGE,
PEELED AND SEGMENTED

1 TEASPOON APPLE CIDER VINEGAR

¼ TEASPOON GROUND CINNAMON

Prepare all the ingredients by rinsing, scrubbing, or peeling as necessary. Cut the ingredients to a size appropriate for your juicer. Process the lettuce, apple, orange, and vinegar. Add the cinnamon, stir, and enjoy.

Variation tip: *Pear cider may not be as ubiquitous as apple cider, but this drink is also delicious when made with a pear.*

Endive Apple Endurance

SERVES

1

PREP TIME: **10 MINUTES**   JUICE TIME: **5 MINUTES**

Do you suffer from mid-afternoon slumps? Think of this juice as a life preserver, providing energy and endurance to power you through your day. Endive is rich in vitamin K, which helps the body properly absorb and store calcium. Endive also contains vitamin A, essential for good eyesight. Lastly, endive is rich in folate, a B vitamin essential during pregnancy and that helps the body repair and build cells. Green apples offer a boost of energy. Chia seeds are known to support healthy energy levels because of their balance of protein, fiber, and healthy fats.

2 HEADS ENDIVE   1 CUCUMBER

2 GREEN APPLES, CORED   1 TABLESPOON CHIA SEEDS

Prepare all the ingredients by rinsing, scrubbing, or peeling as necessary. Cut the ingredients to a size appropriate for your juicer. Process all the ingredients in the juicer, and enjoy within 1 hour.

Ingredient tip: *If you find the quantity of juice yielded is less than expected, juice an additional water-dense vegetable with a mild flavor, such as romaine lettuce or cucumber.*

Tropical Zinger

SERVES

1

PREP TIME: **10 MINUTES**   JUICE TIME: **5 MINUTES**

Need a break? Sipping this juice may transport you to a tropical paradise! Mango and pineapple are two delicious tropical fruits loaded with natural sweetness. The cayenne adds a fun zing as well as mighty health benefits. Did you know that cayenne might serve as a natural remedy for headaches, support detoxification, and boost metabolism? Cilantro is also known to help naturally cleanse the body of heavy metals and toxins.

5 CUPS ROMAINE LETTUCE

1 MANGO, PEELED AND PITTED

1 LEMON

1 (1-INCH) PIECE FRESH GINGER

½ CUP PINEAPPLE

¼ CUP FRESH CILANTRO

PINCH CAYENNE PEPPER

Prepare all the ingredients by rinsing, scrubbing, or peeling as necessary. Cut the ingredients to a size appropriate for your juicer. Process all the ingredients in the juicer, and enjoy.

Timesaving tip: *Prep multiple servings of juice at once! A good-quality juicer can help extend juice life for up to 72 hours when refrigerated in an airtight container (see Types of Juicers, page 16).*

Beet Brain Fog

LOW SUGAR // VEGGIE BASED

SERVES

1

PREP TIME: **10 MINUTES**   JUICE TIME: **5 MINUTES**

Between work, doing laundry, grocery shopping, meal planning, running errands, attending family matters, and staying active, who has time for brain fog? Look to this juice as your new BFF with which to sip your way through a productive day, adding clarity and pep in your step. Beets add bold flavor and rich, beautiful color to this juice, as well as natural sweetness. Beets are also high in antioxidants and contain magnesium, potassium, copper, folate, and even a little protein. The apple, cucumber, and romaine are hydrating fruits and veggies—and hydration is essential for optimal cognitive function.

5 CUPS ROMAINE LETTUCE   1 GREEN APPLE, CORED

1 CUCUMBER   1 LEMON

1 BEET

Prepare all the ingredients by rinsing, scrubbing, or peeling as necessary. Cut the ingredients to a size appropriate for your juicer. Process all the ingredients in the juicer, and enjoy within 1 hour.

Ingredient tip: *Beets can stain your cups or kitchenware, so wash your juice equipment well, and look out for drips of beet juice on your counter.*

Hot Pink Power Juice

FRUIT BASED

SERVES

1

PREP TIME: **10 MINUTES**   JUICE TIME: **5 MINUTES**

This juice is a vibrant pink thanks to dragon fruit, which is rich in phytonutrients and flavonoids. Some dragon fruits are white on the inside and others are pink, so look for pink ones if you're counting on that hot-pink juice. If you can't find dragon fruit at the grocery store, you can replace it with any tropical, water-dense fruit such as pineapple or mango. Regardless of your choice of fruit, this juice will treat you to a sweet and hydrating combo that will naturally boost your energy levels.

5 CUPS ROMAINE LETTUCE   1 BEET

1 CUCUMBER   1 GREEN APPLE, CORED

1 PINK DRAGON FRUIT, PEELED   1 LEMON

Prepare all the ingredients by rinsing, scrubbing, or peeling as necessary. Cut the ingredients to a size appropriate for your juicer. Process all the ingredients in the juicer, and enjoy within 1 hour.

Ingredient tip: *If your fingers turn pink or orange from all your juice-prep, welcome to the club! A natural exfoliator made from sugar and water can help your skin return to its natural shade.*

Citrus Booster

SERVES

1

PREP TIME: **10 MINUTES**   JUICE TIME: **5 MINUTES**

Citrus fruits are perfect for juicing because they're water-dense, incredibly versatile, and easy to pair with so many other fruits and veggies. Citrus fruits are also excellent natural energy boosters. Grapefruit in particular contains an enzyme known as AMP-activated protein kinase (AMPK), which has been known to support weight loss and boost metabolism and energy levels. As always, a water-dense juice means a ramp-up in energy, so this juice also contains several strategic cups of romaine as well as some green apple.

5 CUPS ROMAINE LETTUCE

1 GRAPEFRUIT,
PEELED AND SEGMENTED

1 NAVEL ORANGE,
PEELED AND SEGMENTED

1 GREEN APPLE, CORED

Prepare all the ingredients by rinsing, scrubbing, or peeling as necessary. Cut the ingredients to a size appropriate for your juicer. Process all the ingredients in the juicer, and enjoy.

Ingredient tip: *Depending on the type of juicer you own, this juice may keep for up to 72 hours (see Types of Juicers, page 16). When you store juice, do so in an airtight container in the refrigerator or freezer. Avoid storing in the refrigerator door, as this area experiences more warmth and light (as the door opens and closes) than the refrigerator shelves.*

Watermelon Chia

SERVES

1

PREP TIME: **10 MINUTES**   JUICE TIME: **5 MINUTES**

By now, you likely have noticed a recurring theme—hydration is key for sustaining optimal energy levels! Proper hydration is one of the easiest and most impactful ways to feel your best and help your body thrive. Enter watermelon, which is 92 percent water, and also contains some natural sweetness. Romaine lettuce is another juicing staple. Tasty as well as water-dense, romaine helps increase juice yield. Finally, the chia seeds contain beneficial omega-3 fats and fiber, and they expand massively in liquid, helping boost and stabilize energy levels.

5 CUPS ROMAINE LETTUCE   1 TABLESPOON CHIA SEEDS

3 CUPS WATERMELON

Prepare all the ingredients by rinsing, scrubbing, or peeling as necessary. Cut the ingredients to a size appropriate for your juicer. Process all the ingredients in the juicer, and enjoy within 1 hour.

Ingredient tip: *Be sure to use whole chia seeds, not ground, for this recipe, as this will affect the outcome.*

Hydration Elation

BLENDED JUICE

SERVES

1

PREP TIME: **10 MINUTES**   BLEND TIME: **1 MINUTE**

Do you feel like you're about to fall asleep, yet you still have a long list of to-dos left? Don't reach for an artificial energy drink or coffee, which injects the body with a boost of false energy followed by a sudden crash. Here, watermelon, cucumber, romaine, and apple combine their water-dense superpowers to hydrate and boost brainpower. They also contain essential micronutrients that the body needs to function at an optimal level.

½ CUP FILTERED WATER

1 CUP ROMAINE LETTUCE

1 CUP CABBAGE

1 CUP WATERMELON

1 CUCUMBER

½ GREEN APPLE, CORED

1 LEMON

½ CUP ICE

Prepare all the ingredients by rinsing, scrubbing, or peeling as necessary. Cut the ingredients to a size appropriate for your blender. Add all the ingredients to the blender, following the general principle of liquid first, lightweight ingredients next, and heaviest items on top. Blend on high for 40 to 60 seconds, and enjoy within 1 hour, or refrigerate or freeze overnight.

Ingredient tip: When making blended drinks, you can use filtered water, fresh homemade juice, unsweetened nondairy milks, or coconut water. Filtered water avoids common contaminants found in tap water, such as heavy metals.

Citrus Cherry

BLENDED JUICE

FRUIT BASED

SERVES

1

PREP TIME: **10 MINUTES**   BLEND TIME: **1 MINUTE**

This blended juice features a delicious orange-cherry flavor and a mesmerizing vibrant color. Cherries are high in fiber and an excellent source of vitamin C, potassium, and antioxidants. Cherries have also been known to reduce inflammation, support heart health, and help maintain a healthy weight.

½ CUP FILTERED WATER

1 CUP ROMAINE LETTUCE

1 CUCUMBER

1 NAVEL ORANGE,
PEELED AND SEGMENTED

½ CUP CHERRIES, PITTED

½ CUP ICE

Prepare all the ingredients by rinsing, scrubbing, or peeling as necessary. Cut the ingredients to a size appropriate for your blender. Add all the ingredients to the blender, following the general principle of liquid first, lightweight ingredients next, and heaviest items on top. Blend on high for 40 to 60 seconds, and enjoy.

Ingredient tip: *Pit and freeze cherries when they are in season to have access to this "cherr-ished" fruit all year long!*

Serving tip: *Blended drinks can be made the night before and stored in the refrigerator or freezer. Just give your beverage a good shake or blend again before enjoying.*

Creamy Carrot

BLENDED JUICE

SERVES

1

PREP TIME: **10 MINUTES**   BLEND TIME: **1 MINUTE**

This creamy juice is a light, flavorful beverage with serious kid appeal! Along with fiber, carrots contain vitamins A, C, K, and B$_6$, plus folate and beta-carotene. Vitamin A and beta-carotene support eye health and reduce memory loss. Bananas aid in digestion and contain prebiotics, which support probiotics and the growth of healthy gut bacteria. Poor digestive health can lead to chronic fatigue, and this blended juice is a wonderful step to improve your overall health.

1 CUP FILTERED WATER

1 (1-INCH) PIECE FRESH
GINGER, PEELED

2 CARROTS

1 BANANA, PEELED AND FROZEN

½ LEMON

½ CUP ICE

Prepare all the ingredients by rinsing, scrubbing, or peeling as necessary. Cut the ingredients to a size appropriate for your blender. Add all the ingredients to the blender, following the general principle of liquid first, lightweight ingredients next, and heaviest items on top. Blend on high for 40 to 60 seconds, and enjoy within 1 hour, or refrigerate or freeze overnight.

Ingredient tip: *Instead of adding whole carrots, you can juice the carrots first and add the juice to this recipe. This will result in an even creamier drink. Alternatively, in place of the carrots and water, use 1 cup of fresh carrot juice.*

Coconut Kale

BLENDED JUICE

FRUIT BASED

SERVES

1

PREP TIME: **10 MINUTES**   BLEND TIME: **1 MINUTE**

Blended juices offer a creative way to enjoy the health benefits of fruits and veggies, including their fiber, which is integral for healthy digestion and regular bowel movements. If you notice a dip in your energy multiple times throughout the day, you may want to increase your fiber intake at each meal or snack to sustain your energy levels. This blended juice delivers fiber and healthy fats from the young coconut meat. Coconuts contain a type of medium-chain triglyceride (MCT) that is quickly digested and is a super source of energy.

½ CUP COCONUT WATER

2 CUPS KALE

1 CUCUMBER

¼ CUP YOUNG COCONUT MEAT

1 GREEN APPLE, CORED

½ LEMON, PEELED

½ CUP ICE

Prepare all the ingredients by rinsing, scrubbing, or peeling as necessary. Cut the ingredients to a size appropriate for your blender. Add all the ingredients to the blender, following the general principle of liquid first, lightweight ingredients next, and heaviest items on top. Blend on high for 40 to 60 seconds, and enjoy within 1 hour, or refrigerate or freeze overnight.

Timesaving tip: *For convenience, look for packs of frozen coconut meat in the freezer aisle at the grocery store.*

Coconut Orange Chia

BLENDED JUICE

SERVES

1

PREP TIME: **10 MINUTES**   BLEND TIME: **1 MINUTE**

This blended drink feels like you're sitting poolside on a relaxing vacation. You can get fresh young coconut meat by buying a young brown coconut and scooping out the meat yourself. Alternatively, you can check the frozen section of your grocery store for quality frozen coconut meat, to save the time and effort of whacking open a coconut. Ginger and turmeric explode with flavor, adding valuable health benefits by improving blood circulation and digestion.

½ CUP COCONUT WATER

1 TABLESPOON CHIA SEEDS

1 (½-INCH) PIECE FRESH
GINGER, PEELED

1 (½-INCH) PIECE FRESH
TURMERIC, PEELED

1 NAVEL ORANGE,
PEELED AND SEGMENTED

¼ CUP YOUNG COCONUT MEAT
(FRESH OR FROZEN)

1 BANANA, PEELED AND FROZEN

½ CUP ICE

Prepare all the ingredients by rinsing, scrubbing, or peeling as necessary. Cut the ingredients to a size appropriate for your blender. Add all the ingredients to the blender, following the general principle of liquid first, lightweight ingredients next, and heaviest items on top. Blend on high for 40 to 60 seconds, and enjoy within 1 hour, or refrigerate or freeze overnight.

Timesaving tip: *Peel and slice ripe bananas, and store them in a container in the freezer. This way, you'll always have bananas on hand to make delicious creamy blended drinks.*

Immune System Support

Orange You Glad

SERVES

1

Sheer happiness in a cup—and once you make this juice, you'll see why! It's colorful, flavorful, and a nutritional powerhouse. Oranges contain vitamin C as well as vitamins A and B6, plus calcium and potassium. I love adding turmeric to all sorts of recipes, and its inherent curcumin—a compound with anti-inflammatory and antioxidant properties—certainly makes it a valuable juicing add-in. Some studies have shown that curcumin may be beneficial in treating and managing arthritis pain. Additionally, the ginger in this happy drink may alleviate nausea or relieve an upset stomach.

2 LARGE CARROTS

1 NAVEL ORANGE,
PEELED AND SEGMENTED

1 APPLE, CORED

1 (1-INCH) PIECE FRESH GINGER

1 (1-INCH) PIECE FRESH TURMERIC

Prepare all the ingredients by rinsing, scrubbing, or peeling as necessary. Cut the ingredients to a size appropriate for your juicer. Process all the ingredients in the juicer, and enjoy within 1 hour.

Serving tip: *If you can't drink your juice right away, transfer it to an ice cube tray and freeze. This will allow you to use it in recipes at a later time.*

Timesaving tip: *Depending on the type of juicer you own, you can store this juice in the refrigerator and enjoy within up to 72 hours (see Types of Juicers, page 16).*

Super C

SERVES

1

PREP TIME: **10 MINUTES**   JUICE TIME: **5 MINUTES**

Oranges are automatically associated with vitamin C, but lemons, kiwis, apples, and bell peppers are also terrific sources. In fact, one kiwi has four times the vitamin C of an orange. Kiwis are also a great low-sugar, low-glycemic fruit loaded with antioxidants. To boot, the lemon in this drink delivers approximately 50 percent of your daily recommended intake of vitamin C. Clearly, we've got ourselves a Super C!

5 CUPS ROMAINE LETTUCE

1 CUCUMBER

1 YELLOW BELL PEPPER, CORED

1 NAVEL ORANGE,
PEELED AND SEGMENTED

1 GREEN APPLE, CORED

1 LEMON

1 KIWI

Prepare all the ingredients by rinsing, scrubbing, or peeling as necessary. Cut the ingredients to a size appropriate for your juicer. Process all the ingredients in the juicer, and enjoy within 1 hour.

Ingredient tip: *If your pulp is still damp, you can re-juice the pulp to maximize yield and nutrition.*

Bloat Buster

GREEN JUICE // LOW SUGAR // VEGGIE BASED

SERVES

1

PREP TIME: **10 MINUTES**   JUICE TIME: **5 MINUTES**

Whether it's related to hormone fluctuations or dietary distress, feeling bloated is a real downer. Symptoms of dehydration include a slow, sluggish metabolism as well as gas and bloating. Enter fennel, a powerful herb known to help reduce the discomforts of gas and bloating. Try some in this hydrating juice, which is packed with bloat-busting ingredients. The lemon and ginger aid in digestion, and the water-dense romaine lettuce, cucumbers, and celery reduce bloat. All together, they aim to help your tummy feel better!

5 CUPS ROMAINE LETTUCE

2 CUCUMBERS

2 CELERY STALKS

¼ CUP FENNEL

1 LEMON

1 (1-INCH) PIECE FRESH GINGER

Prepare all the ingredients by rinsing, scrubbing, or peeling as necessary. Cut the ingredients to a size appropriate for your juicer. Process all the ingredients in the juicer, and enjoy within 1 hour.

Ingredient tip: *You can juice the bulb, stalks, and fronds (feathery leaves) of the fennel; it's all good!*

Heal and Hydrate

GREEN JUICE // LOW SUGAR // VEGGIE BASED

SERVES

1

PREP TIME: **10 MINUTES**   JUICE TIME: **5 MINUTES**

Sip your way to myriad health benefits with this simple, nourishing green juice. Spinach contains flavonoids that act as antioxidants, which can help fight free radicals. Left unchecked, free radicals harm the body's healthy cells and accelerate the aging process. Spinach is also rich in folate, an important nutrient that may support healthy heart function, and magnesium, an essential mineral that can help lower blood pressure levels and reduce symptoms of anxiety. Ginger supports circulation and digestion. And turmeric contains a compound known as curcumin, which delivers anti-inflammatory benefits.

5 CUPS SPINACH

2 CUCUMBERS

1 PEAR, CORED

1 LEMON

1 (½-INCH) PIECE FRESH GINGER

1 (½-INCH) PIECE FRESH TURMERIC

Prepare all the ingredients by rinsing, scrubbing, or peeling as necessary. Cut the ingredients to a size appropriate for your juicer. Process all the ingredients in the juicer, and enjoy within 1 hour.

Ingredient tip: *When juicing pears and apples, you can juice the core as well; just make sure to discard the stem and seeds.*

Ginger Garlic Goodness

GREEN JUICE // VEGGIE BASED

SERVES

1

PREP TIME: **10 MINUTES**   JUICE TIME: **5 MINUTES**

This sweet and tangy juice with a hint of garlic will awaken your taste buds and sharpen your senses! Garlic possesses extraordinary anti-bacterial, antifungal, and anti-inflammatory properties. And masking the pungent flavor profile are some additional tasty ingredients: Green apples add natural sweetness, while lemons, romaine lettuce, spinach, and ginger add immune-boosting nutrients like vitamin C.

3 CUPS ROMAINE LETTUCE

3 CUPS SPINACH

2 GREEN APPLES, CORED

1 LEMON

1 (1-INCH) PIECE FRESH GINGER

1 GARLIC CLOVE

Prepare all the ingredients by rinsing, scrubbing, or peeling as necessary. Cut the ingredients to a size appropriate for your juicer. Process all the ingredients in the juicer, and enjoy within 1 hour.

Health tip: *This is a fantastic juice to drink if you've caught a cold or are feeling under the weather—unless, of course, you are a vampire!*

Fruity Fennel

FRUIT BASED

SERVES

1

PREP TIME: **10 MINUTES**   JUICE TIME: **5 MINUTES**

Cold and flu season upon you? Studies show that the body's immune system is intimately linked with gut health. Fennel is a wonderful herb for supporting digestive health and reducing gas and bloating. This juice also contains some navel orange, apple, and lemon for a hefty dose of antioxidant vitamin C. So let this juice work its magic on you, and be confident you've consumed something smart—and tasty—to protect yourself from illness.

5 CUPS ROMAINE LETTUCE

1 NAVEL ORANGE, PEELED AND SEGMENTED

1 GREEN APPLE, CORED

1 LEMON

¼ CUP FENNEL

Prepare all the ingredients by rinsing, scrubbing, or peeling as necessary. Cut the ingredients to a size appropriate for your juicer. Process all the ingredients in the juicer, and enjoy within 1 hour.

Ingredient tip: *Fennel has a licorice taste, and a little goes a long way. Feel free to adjust the fennel quantity and taste-test as you go, to avoid an overpowering juice.*

Happy Belly Juice

SERVES

1

PREP TIME: **10 MINUTES**   JUICE TIME: **5 MINUTES**

A happy, healthy belly is vital for overall health! Dandelion greens and ginger are both key players supporting belly health. Blueberries are a low-sugar fruit with loads of benefits, including their ability to reduce the gas or flatulence that some people may experience from a high-sugar diet. The lemons in this juice are also great for digestive health, effectively relieving indigestion and upset stomach. The enzymes in lemons help stimulate the liver, the body's main detox organ, to flush out toxins.

5 CUPS ROMAINE LETTUCE

1 CUP DANDELION GREENS

1 CUP BLUEBERRIES

1 CUCUMBER

1 LEMON

1 (1-INCH) PIECE FRESH GINGER

Prepare all the ingredients by rinsing, scrubbing, or peeling as necessary. Cut the ingredients to a size appropriate for your juicer. Process all the ingredients in the juicer, and enjoy within 1 hour.

Variation tip: *If this juice is too tangy for you, try adding an apple for natural sweetness.*

Antioxidant Juice

FRUIT BASED

SERVES

1

PREP TIME: **10 MINUTES**   JUICE TIME: **5 MINUTES**

Antioxidants inhibit oxidation, effectively benefiting the human body by neutralizing and removing free radicals. A free radical is an uncharged molecule that is highly reactive and can have negative effects on your body's healthy cells. To combat this, fruits, vegetables, herbs, and spices are wonderful sources of antioxidants. This juice in particular is antioxidant-rich, thanks to its abundance of blueberries, kale, lemon, and ginger.

3 CUPS ROMAINE LETTUCE

3 CUPS KALE

1 CUP BLUEBERRIES

1 CUCUMBER

1 GREEN APPLE, CORED

1 LEMON

1 (1-INCH) PIECE FRESH GINGER

Prepare all the ingredients by rinsing, scrubbing, or peeling as necessary. Cut the ingredients to a size appropriate for your juicer. Process all the ingredients in the juicer, and enjoy.

Timesaving tip: *Depending on the type of juicer you own, you can often make a double or triple batch of this juice and refrigerate for up to 72 hours (see Types of Juicers, page 16).*

Cilantro Sipper

GREEN JUICE // VEGGIE BASED

SERVES

1

PREP TIME: **10 MINUTES**   JUICE TIME: **5 MINUTES**

We are all exposed to toxins and heavy metals every day, whether from tap water, beauty products, or fumes from pollution. While we can limit or reduce our exposure to some sources, others are just part of life. It is also within our power to cleanse and detoxify by consuming fruits, vegetables, herbs, and spices that support the liver, our main detox organ. To this end, cilantro is one of the best herbs to consume because it binds to heavy metals and helps excrete them from our system. To offset the strong cilantro flavor, this juice contains sweet and tangy lemon, apples, and romaine lettuce.

5 CUPS ROMAINE LETTUCE

3 CELERY STALKS

2 GREEN APPLES, CORED

1 LEMON

½ CUP FRESH CILANTRO

Prepare all the ingredients by rinsing, scrubbing, or peeling as necessary. Cut the ingredients to a size appropriate for your juicer. Process all the ingredients in the juicer, and enjoy within 1 hour.

Substitution tip: *Some people just don't like cilantro—no problem! Swap it out for parsley or another leafy green.*

Get Well Juice

SERVES

1

PREP TIME: **10 MINUTES**   JUICE TIME: **5 MINUTES**

You know that awful feeling where you think you're coming down with a cold? When you're starting to feel off, fresh homemade juice is an excellent way to flood your system with immune-boosting nutrients. This juice contains a variety of vitamin C–rich fruits such as lemon, lime, apple, and orange. Ginger is also great if your stomach feels off, because this aromatic spice can help improve digestion. When you're under the weather, the more greens, the better—and this juice obliges with romaine lettuce, cabbage, and digestion-boosting dandelion greens.

2 CUPS ROMAINE LETTUCE

2 CUPS CABBAGE

1 CUP DANDELION GREENS

1 NAVEL ORANGE,
PEELED AND SEGMENTED

1 GREEN APPLE, CORED

1 LEMON

1 LIME

1 (1-INCH) PIECE FRESH GINGER

Prepare all the ingredients by rinsing, scrubbing, or peeling as necessary. Cut the ingredients to a size appropriate for your juicer. Process all the ingredients in the juicer, and enjoy within 1 hour.

Health tip: *If you have leftover juice, it can be stored as ice cubes and tossed into a smoothie or used to chill another juice for a boost of nutrition!*

Tropical Turmeric Juice

BLENDED JUICE

FRUIT BASED

SERVES

1

PREP TIME: **10 MINUTES**   BLEND TIME: **1 MINUTE**

I am obsessed with turmeric. It's so incredibly nutritious, and adds a vibrant color to any recipe, like this tropical turmeric smoothie. And I probably don't have to sell you on the other ingredients. This blended beverage is super sweet from the pineapple, mango, and banana—satisfying your sweet tooth, perfectly and guiltlessly. And the coconut, not to be outdone, contains lauric acid and caprylic acid, both of which have antifungal and antibacterial properties, supporting a healthy, strong immune system. Try this and be transported to the tropics!

1 CUP COCONUT WATER

1 (1-INCH) PIECE FRESH TURMERIC, PEELED

1 MANGO, PEELED AND PITTED

½ CUP PINEAPPLE

¼ CUP YOUNG COCONUT MEAT (FRESH OR FROZEN)

1 BANANA, PEELED AND FROZEN

½ CUP ICE

Prepare all the ingredients by rinsing, scrubbing, or peeling as necessary. Cut the ingredients to a size appropriate for your blender. Add all the ingredients to the blender, following the general principle of liquid first, lightweight ingredients next, and heaviest items on top. Blend on high for 40 to 60 seconds, and enjoy within 1 hour, or refrigerate or freeze overnight.

Substitution tip: *If you don't have fresh turmeric, you can use ⅛ teaspoon of ground. While you're at it, feel free to adjust the amounts to meet your taste preferences.*

Rooted in Health

BLENDED JUICE

FRUIT BASED

SERVES

1

PREP TIME: **10 MINUTES**   BLEND TIME: **1 MINUTE**

You'll probably find a favorite juice combination that you want to make again and again. This is one of my favorites. It's sweet enough to be a treat, so it's perfect for mid-afternoon when I'm craving something sweet yet am also in need of an energy boost. It's packed with immune-supportive ingredients such as lemon, pineapple, and rainbow chard. Blended drinks are loaded with fiber, so they make a great go-to when you want to hydrate and satisfy your hunger at the same time.

½ CUP FILTERED WATER

1 TEASPOON GROUND FLAXSEED

2 CUPS RAINBOW CHARD

1 CUCUMBER

½ CUP PINEAPPLE

1 BANANA, PEELED AND FROZEN

1 LEMON

½ CUP ICE

Prepare all the ingredients by rinsing, scrubbing, or peeling as necessary. Cut the ingredients to a size appropriate for your blender. Add all the ingredients to the blender, following the general principle of liquid first, lightweight ingredients next, and heaviest items on top. Blend on high for 40 to 60 seconds, and enjoy within 1 hour, or refrigerate or freeze overnight.

Ingredient tip: *When making blended drinks, you can use filtered water, fresh homemade juice, unsweetened nondairy milks, or coconut water. Filtered water avoids common contaminants found in tap water, such as heavy metals.*

Parsley Power

BLENDED JUICE

FRUIT BASED

SERVES

1

PREP TIME: **10 MINUTES**   BLEND TIME: **1 MINUTE**

Parsley is a powerful herb that contains a variety of antioxidants including luteolin, apigenin, lycopene, beta-carotene, and alpha-carotene. These antioxidants may help fight free radicals and inflammation. When blended with creamy, sweet banana, the parsley flavor diminishes. Cucumber and romaine are hydrating vegetables, and proper hydration has a huge impact on immune health. Staying hydrated helps your blood carry oxygen to all the cells in your body, so your organs and systems can thrive.

1 CUP FILTERED WATER

¼ CUP FRESH PARSLEY

2 CUPS ROMAINE LETTUCE

1 CUCUMBER

1 BANANA, PEELED AND FROZEN

½ CUP ICE

Prepare all the ingredients by rinsing, scrubbing, or peeling as necessary. Cut the ingredients to a size appropriate for your blender. Add all the ingredients to the blender, following the general principle of liquid first, lightweight ingredients next, and heaviest items on top. Blend on high for 40 to 60 seconds, and enjoy, or refrigerate or freeze overnight.

Variation tip: *Bananas, dates, apples, and raw local honey are just a few great natural sweeteners to add to blended juices—they can help mask the strong flavor profiles of greens and herbs.*

Healing Greens

BLENDED JUICE

GREEN JUICE // GUT HEALTH // VEGGIE BASED

SERVES

1

PREP TIME: **10 MINUTES**   BLEND TIME: **1 MINUTE**

The best foods for boosting immune health are plant-based foods high in vitamins, minerals, antioxidants, phytonutrients, and fiber. Dandelion greens, lemons, ginger, and turmeric are excellent choices for helping the body heal and repair.

1 CUP FILTERED WATER

2 CUPS SPINACH

1 CUP DANDELION GREENS

¼ CUP FRESH PARSLEY

1 (½-INCH) PIECE FRESH GINGER, PEELED

1 (½-INCH) PIECE FRESH TURMERIC, PEELED

½ LEMON

1 BANANA, PEELED AND FROZEN

½ CUP ICE

Prepare all the ingredients by rinsing, scrubbing, or peeling as necessary. Cut the ingredients to a size appropriate for your blender. Add all the ingredients to the blender, following the general principle of liquid first, lightweight ingredients next, and heaviest items on top. Blend on high for 40 to 60 seconds, and enjoy.

Serving tip: *Blended drinks can be made the night before and stored in the refrigerator or freezer. Give your beverage a good shake or blend again before enjoying!*

Blackberry Mint

BLENDED JUICE

FRUIT BASED

SERVES

1

PREP TIME: **10 MINUTES**   BLEND TIME: **1 MINUTE**

An old folk remedy preaches that blackberries may block the flu virus. More research is needed to confirm the validity, but in the meantime, it definitely doesn't hurt to eat more blackberries! Blackberries contain vitamin C and infection-fighting antioxidants, plus folate, manganese, vitamin K, copper, vitamin E, potassium, and magnesium. This juice features several delicious and beneficial foods, including mint, a wonderful herb that supports digestive health and can help alleviate an upset stomach.

1 CUP COCONUT WATER

¼ CUP FRESH MINT

1 CUP BLACKBERRIES, FRESH OR FROZEN

¼ AVOCADO, PEELED AND PITTED

¼ CUP YOUNG COCONUT MEAT (FRESH OR FROZEN)

½ LEMON

1 BANANA, PEELED AND FROZEN

½ CUP ICE

Prepare all the ingredients by rinsing, scrubbing, or peeling as necessary. Cut the ingredients to a size appropriate for your blender. Add all the ingredients to the blender, following the general principle of liquid first, lightweight ingredients next, and heaviest items on top. Blend on high for 40 to 60 seconds, and enjoy within 1 hour, or refrigerate or freeze overnight.

Variation tip: *Fresh or frozen berries can be used in this recipe as well as in any blended recipe in this book.*

9

Plant-Based Suppers

Garden Vegetable Soup

SERVES

4

PREP TIME: **10 MINUTES**   COOK TIME: **30 MINUTES**

Soup is warm, comforting, and nourishing, and the leftovers are even better! Soup is one of my favorite dishes to make. If you don't have much experience with soup recipes, I'd like to reassure you that homemade vegetable soup is simple to make, and you can easily adjust your ingredients to use whatever you have on hand. One of my tricks for making homemade soup is using veggie stems, which often get tossed or composted. In particular, I love to chop and blend broccoli stems and add them to the soup broth for an extra boost of vitamins and minerals.

1 TABLESPOON COCONUT OIL

½ SMALL RED ONION, CHOPPED

3 GARLIC CLOVES, MINCED

4 CUPS VEGETABLE BROTH, DIVIDED

1 SMALL HEAD BROCCOLI,
STEMS AND FLORETS SEPARATED,
STEMS CHOPPED

1 (1-INCH) PIECE FRESH GINGER,
PEELED AND DICED

1 (1-INCH) PIECE FRESH TURMERIC,
PEELED AND DICED

5 CUPS KALE

2 LARGE CARROTS,
ROUGHLY CHOPPED

2 CELERY STALKS, ROUGHLY CHOPPED

1 MEDIUM RUSSET POTATO, UNPEELED,
SCRUBBED AND ROUGHLY CHOPPED

½ CUP PEAS

1. In a deep sauté pan or soup pot over medium heat, add the coconut oil and onion. Cook until the onion has browned, about 5 minutes, stirring occasionally.

2. Add the garlic and cook for another 3 minutes, stirring occasionally.

3. Meanwhile, in a blender, combine 1 cup of broth, the broccoli stems, ginger, and turmeric, and blend until liquefied.

4. Add the broth-broccoli mixture and the remaining 3 cups of broth to the pan.

5. Add the broccoli florets, kale, carrots, celery, potato, and peas.

6. Cover and simmer for 20 to 30 minutes, stirring occasionally until the potatoes are tender and soup is hot.

Substitution tip: *Feel free to substitute any ingredients for ones you have on hand. For example, the russet potato can be swapped for butternut squash or sweet potato.*

Lemongrass Coconut Noodle Soup

SERVES
4

PREP TIME: **5 MINUTES**   COOK TIME: **40 MINUTES**

This soup is so flavorful and comforting. Anytime I feel a little under the weather, or it's just a cloudy day, this is the soup I crave. You can find brown-rice pad Thai noodles at most grocery stores in the Asian aisle. Bok choy is fantastic in soup. Its stem has a celery-like appearance and crunch, while the leafy greens add calcium, potassium, and vitamin C. This soup can be stored in the refrigerator and enjoyed within two to three days.

1 (1-INCH) PIECE FRESH GINGER, PEELED

1 (1-INCH) PIECE FRESH TURMERIC, PEELED

2 CUPS VEGETABLE BROTH

1 CUP CANNED FULL-FAT COCONUT MILK

JUICE OF 1 LIME

1 TABLESPOON COCONUT OIL

½ RED ONION, THINLY SLICED

1 LARGE HEAD BOK CHOY, CHOPPED

3 LEMONGRASS STALKS, PEELED AND DICED

2 LARGE CARROTS, DICED

2 CELERY STALKS, DICED

4 OUNCES BROWN-RICE PAD THAI NOODLES

SEA SALT

2 TABLESPOONS FRESH CILANTRO LEAVES

1. In a blender, combine the ginger, turmeric, broth, coconut milk, and lime juice, and blend on high for 1 minute.

2. In a deep sauté pan or soup pot over medium heat, heat the coconut oil. Add the onion and sauté for 5 minutes, stirring occasionally.

3. Add the ginger-turmeric broth to the pan, and simmer for 20 minutes.

4. Add the bok choy, lemongrass, carrots, celery, and noodles, making sure the noodles are completely covered in liquid, and simmer for 15 minutes. Season with salt.

5. Garnish with the cilantro and an extra squeeze of lime, and serve.

Substitution tip: *Ground turmeric and ginger can be used in place of fresh. Use ⅛ teaspoon of ground in place of 1 inch of fresh. Feel free to adjust to your taste preferences.*

Cauliflower Parsnip Soup

SERVES

4

PREP TIME: **10 MINUTES**   COOK TIME: **35 MINUTES**

Creamy blended soups feel decadent, as if you're dining at a five-star restaurant. But in reality, they are quick, budget-friendly meals! Parsnips are a root vegetable closely related to carrots. They are high in fiber and also contain plenty of potassium, manganese, magnesium, phosphorus, and iron. Cauliflower is a cruciferous vegetable that's high in fiber, vitamin C, and antioxidants to fight inflammation.

1 TABLESPOON COCONUT OIL

1 SMALL YELLOW ONION, DICED

3 GARLIC CLOVES, MINCED

1 (1-INCH) PIECE FRESH TURMERIC, DICED

PINCH SEA SALT

2 CUPS PEELED CHOPPED PARSNIPS

1 CAULIFLOWER HEAD, CHOPPED

2 CUPS SPINACH

4 CUPS VEGETABLE BROTH

½ CUP CANNED COCONUT MILK

1. In a deep sauté pan or soup pot over medium heat, heat the coconut oil. Add the onion and cook until the onion has browned, about 5 minutes, stirring occasionally.

2. Add the garlic, turmeric, and salt, and cook for another 2 minutes.

3. Add the parsnips, cauliflower, spinach, broth, and coconut milk.

4. Bring the soup to a boil, then reduce the heat and simmer for 30 minutes until the parsnips and cauliflower are very tender.

5. Carefully add the soup mixture to a blender and blend until smooth, working in batches if necessary. You can also use an immersion blender.

6. Serve and enjoy.

Substitution tip: *This soup can be made with potatoes or sweet potatoes in place of the parsnips.*

Veggie Lentil Chili

SERVES
4

PREP TIME: **10 MINUTES**   COOK TIME: **30 MINUTES**

If you're a fan of chili, you'll love this flavorful dish packed with protein, especially on a chilly day. Did you know that 1 cup of lentils has 18 grams of protein? Lentils also contain fiber and no cholesterol or saturated fat. This satiating chili is delicious on its own or served over brown rice or with organic crackers or chips.

1 TABLESPOON COCONUT OIL

1 SMALL WHITE ONION, DICED

2 LARGE CARROTS, DICED

2 CELERY STALKS, DICED

3 GARLIC CLOVES, MINCED

2 (15-OUNCE) CANS LENTILS, DRAINED

1 (28-OUNCE) CAN
CRUSHED TOMATOES

2 (4-OUNCE) CANS GREEN
CHILES, DRAINED

¼ CUP CHILI POWDER

2 TABLESPOONS GROUND OREGANO

2 TABLESPOONS FRESHLY GROUND
BLACK PEPPER

2 TABLESPOONS SEA SALT

2 TABLESPOONS GROUND CUMIN

1. In a soup pot over medium heat, heat the coconut oil. Add the onion and cook for about 4 minutes, stirring occasionally, until the onion starts to brown.

2. Add the carrots, celery, and garlic, and cook, stirring occasionally, for another 1 to 2 minutes.

3. Add the lentils, tomatoes, chiles, chili powder, oregano, pepper, salt, and cumin, stirring to blend.

4. Cover and simmer for 20 minutes, stirring occasionally.

5. Serve and enjoy.

Substitution tip: *Lentils are great, but any legume works in this recipe. Try it with white beans, kidney beans, black beans, or a combo.*

Ingredient tip: *When shopping for canned goods, look for the label "BPA-free."*

Zucchini Noodles with Basil Pesto

SERVES

PREP TIME: **5 MINUTES**   COOK TIME: **5 MINUTES**

If you love pasta but are watching your blood sugar levels and limiting your intake of processed carbohydrates, you must try veggie noodles! Vegetables such as zucchini, cucumber, and carrots can be easily spun into noodles using a handy kitchen gadget known as a spiralizer. You can enjoy veggie noodles cold or hot! This pesto is made with plenty of basil, one of my favorite herbs. While traditional pesto contains cheese, this pesto is dairy-free and vegan—a wonderful complement to the Plant-Powered Juicing Plan.

2 ZUCCHINI, ENDS TRIMMED FLAT

2 CUPS FRESH BASIL LEAVES

½ CUP RAW UNSALTED ALMONDS

½ CUP PINE NUTS

½ LEMON

3 TABLESPOONS OLIVE OIL, PLUS MORE IF NEEDED

5 ROASTED GARLIC CLOVES (SEE COOKING TIP)

PINCH SEA SALT

1. Run the zucchini through a spiralizer (or veggie-noodle gadget of choice). Set aside.

2. In a food processor, combine the basil, almonds, pine nuts, lemon, olive oil, garlic, and salt, and pulse until creamy, adding a bit more oil if necessary.

3. Toss the noodles with the pesto, and enjoy!

Cooking tip: *To roast garlic, peel away the dry skins from the head of garlic, leaving the cloves together. Cut off the tops so you can see the cloves. Drizzle with 2 tablespoons of cooking oil, cover, and bake in a 425°F oven for 15 to 20 minutes. Once cooled, push the cloves out.*

Substitution tip: *Almonds and pine nuts can be expensive. For a budget-friendly pesto, omit the pine nuts and increase the amount of almonds, or use walnuts or pecans instead.*

Carrot Noodle and Snap Pea Salad

SERVES

PREP TIME: **10 MINUTES**   COOK TIME: **0 MINUTES**

This colorful salad is crunchy, bright, and delicious. It also holds up well in the refrigerator (with the dressing on the side) if you like to prep your lunch the night before and take it to work with you the next day. If you're not a fan of bell peppers or snap peas, top the carrot noodles with an endless variety of fresh crunchy vegetables, such as fire-roasted corn and red onion.

4 LARGE CARROTS, PEELED, AND ENDS TRIMMED FLAT

1 (15-OUNCE) CAN CHICKPEAS, DRAINED AND RINSED

1 GREEN BELL PEPPER, CHOPPED

1 CUP SNAP PEAS

2 TABLESPOONS FRESH CILANTRO

2 TABLESPOONS SESAME SEEDS

JUICE OF 1 LEMON

¼ CUP OLIVE OIL

1 TABLESPOON MAPLE SYRUP OR RAW LOCAL HONEY

1 TABLESPOON TAHINI

1 TEASPOON ONION POWDER

1 TEASPOON GARLIC POWDER

1. Run the carrots through a spiralizer (or veggie-noodle gadget of choice). Transfer to a medium bowl.

2. Add the chickpeas, bell pepper, snap peas, cilantro, and sesame seeds to the bowl with the carrots.

3. In a small bowl, whisk together the lemon juice, olive oil, maple syrup, tahini, onion powder, and garlic powder.

4. Just before serving, toss the salad with the salad dressing.

5. Top the salad with the cilantro and sesame seeds, and enjoy!

Kale Caesar Quinoa Salad

SERVES

PREP TIME: **10 MINUTES**   COOK TIME: **0 MINUTES**

This recipe has all the delicious flavors of a traditional Caesar, but it's vegan and gluten-free! Tahini, made from ground sesame seeds, can be found in the nut-butter aisle next to all the peanut butters and almond butters. Tahini has a very strong flavor profile, so unlike peanut butter, it's not an ideal spread. But it is a wonderful ingredient in homemade salad dressings or sauces, adding protein and a thick creamy texture. Quinoa is also great in this salad for even more protein and a boost of fiber.

½ CUP OLIVE OIL

2 TABLESPOONS FRESHLY SQUEEZED LEMON JUICE

6 ROASTED GARLIC CLOVES (SEE COOKING TIP)

1 TABLESPOON TAHINI

PINCH SEA SALT

4 CUPS CHOPPED KALE, STEMS REMOVED

½ CUP COOKED QUINOA

2 TABLESPOONS HEMP SEEDS

1 TABLESPOON CAPERS

1 FRESH RIPE AVOCADO, PEELED, PITTED, AND SLICED

1. In a blender, blend the olive oil, lemon juice, garlic, tahini, and salt until creamy. Set aside.

2. In a large bowl, add kale and 2 to 4 tablespoons of salad dressing. Massage kale with clean hands to soften the kale, which makes it more palatable.

3. Add quinoa, hemp seeds and capers. Toss all ingredients together.

4. Divide into two bowls, and top with the avocado.

Cooking tip: *To roast garlic, peel away the dry skins from the head of garlic, leaving the cloves together. Cut off the tops so you can see the cloves. Drizzle with 2 tablespoons of cooking oil, cover, and bake in a 425°F oven for 15 to 20 minutes. Once cooled, push the cloves out.*

Variation tip: *Not on the kale train just yet? Give it a try; if it's not for you, romaine lettuce is also delicious in this salad!*

Quinoa Burrito Bowl

SERVES

PREP TIME: **10 MINUTES**   COOK TIME: **20 MINUTES**

This flavorful bowl is sure to be a hit in your house—it's fresh, filling, and delicious. Quinoa is a gluten-free pseudo-grain, meaning it's actually a seed that cooks like a grain. It contains higher levels of protein and fiber than most grains. Of course, the more veggies the better, so this burrito bowl is packed with romaine, cilantro, and tomatoes. Black olives contain healthy monounsaturated fat—the good kind that supports heart and brain health by raising our HDL "good" cholesterol levels. If you're not a fan of olives, simply leave them out.

½ CUP UNCOOKED QUINOA

1 CUP FILTERED WATER

2 CUPS CHOPPED ROMAINE LETTUCE

1 (15-OUNCE) CAN PINTO BEANS, DRAINED AND RINSED

¼ CUP CHERRY TOMATOES, HALVED

1 AVOCADO, PEELED, PITTED, AND SLICED

2 TABLESPOONS BLACK OLIVES, SLICED

2 TABLESPOONS FRESH CILANTRO LEAVES

JUICE OF 1 LIME

¼ CUP FRESH SALSA

1. Cook the quinoa in the water according to the package instructions.

2. In a large bowl, combine the romaine, beans, tomatoes, avocado, olives, cilantro, and lime juice, tossing to blend.

3. Top with the salsa and serve hot.

Variation tip: This bowl is easy to adapt to meet your dietary preferences. You can easily swap brown rice for the quinoa or chickpeas for the pinto beans.

Loaded Sweet Potatoes

SERVES

PREP TIME: **10 MINUTES**   COOK TIME: **60 MINUTES**

If you're worried about calories from potatoes you may be delighted to know that one medium sweet potato contains only 115 calories and 5 grams of fiber. Sweet potatoes contain more fiber and vitamin C than a traditional white potato, serving as a nutritious staple in a plant-powered diet. They are also great paired with a protein like black beans, to avoid blood sugar spikes. The spicy cashew cream sauce for this dish is delicious, really simple to make, and packs some additional protein.

FOR THE CASHEW CREAM SAUCE

½ CUP RAW CASHEWS

1 CUP FILTERED WATER, DIVIDED

1 TABLESPOON FRESHLY SQUEEZED LEMON JUICE

1 TEASPOON ONION POWDER

1 TEASPOON GARLIC POWDER

1 TEASPOON HOT SAUCE

PINCH SEA SALT

FOR THE SWEET POTATOES

2 SWEET POTATOES OR YAMS

1 TABLESPOON COCONUT OIL

½ SMALL ONION, SLICED

1 RED BELL PEPPER, SLICED

1 (15-OUNCE) CAN BLACK BEANS, DRAINED AND RINSED

2 TABLESPOONS FRESH CILANTRO

TO MAKE THE CASHEW CREAM SAUCE

1. Soak the cashews in ½ cup of filtered water overnight.

2. Discard the water. In a food processor or blender, combine the soaked cashews, the remaining ½ cup of water, lemon juice, onion powder, garlic powder, hot sauce, and salt. Blend until smooth and creamy. Set aside.

TO MAKE THE SWEET POTATOES

1. Preheat the oven to 425°F.

2. With a fork, poke holes in the sweet potatoes and bake them for 60 minutes.

3. About 15 minutes before the sweet potatoes are fully cooked, heat a medium sauté pan over medium heat. Add the coconut oil and onion and cook until browned, about 5 minutes, stirring occasionally.

4. Add the bell pepper and cook for another 3 to 5 minutes, stirring occasionally.

5. Add the beans and cook for 2 to 3 minutes, stirring occasionally.

6. Slice the sweet potatoes in half lengthwise.

7. Fill the potatoes with the black-bean mixture, and top with the cilantro and a drizzle of cashew cream sauce.

Ingredient tip: Do beans upset your stomach? Rinse and drain the beans before cooking to help reduce the amount of indigestible sugars. You can also try different beans; you may tolerate some better than others.

Coconut Thai Curry Bowl

SERVES

4

PREP TIME: **10 MINUTES**   COOK TIME: **30 MINUTES**

Whenever I'm craving takeout, this bowl hits the spot—it's flavorful and fills me up, not out! Brown rice is a naturally gluten-free grain that contains fiber and B vitamins. Cabbage is often considered a diet food, but it's incredibly nutritious, and quite delicious when prepared right! Cabbage contains sulfur, known as the "beautifying mineral," because it can help clear up oily and acne-prone skin. Cabbage is also packed with fiber to support healthy digestion and bowel regularity.

1 CUP UNCOOKED BROWN RICE

2 CUPS FILTERED WATER

2 CARROTS, CUT INTO
¼-INCH-THICK ROUNDS

2 CUPS COOKED CHICKPEAS

1 CUP CANNED FULL-FAT
COCONUT MILK

2 TABLESPOONS RED THAI
CURRY PASTE

½ HEAD GREEN CABBAGE,
THINLY SLICED

½ CUP FRESH BASIL LEAVES, MINCED

JUICE OF ½ LIME

2 TEASPOONS HEMP OIL OR OLIVE OIL

1. In a small saucepan over high heat, bring the rice and water to a rapid boil. Cover, and lower the heat to simmer for 30 minutes.

2. In another small saucepan over medium heat, combine the carrots, chickpeas, coconut milk, and curry paste. Bring to a slow boil and then lower the heat to simmer for 20 minutes.

3. In a small bowl, stir together the cabbage, basil, lime juice, and hemp oil until well blended.

4. Transfer the rice to a serving bowl. Pour the curry over the rice and top with the cabbage mixture.

5. Serve hot.

Ingredient tip: *Store cans of coconut milk in the refrigerator; overnight prior to cooking this helps create a thicker, creamier consistency.*

Sweet Potato Cauliflower Tacos

SERVES

PREP TIME: **15 MINUTES**   COOK TIME: **30 MINUTES**

I could eat tacos every week—and we do! Tacos are a great family meal staple because everyone can pick and choose exactly what they want. In this recipe, we use cauliflower, which is chopped super-fine and seasoned with taco seasoning to resemble ground meat—but this meal is of course completely plant-based! Sweet potatoes are an excellent taco filling, and when cut into tiny cubes and roasted, are satisfyingly crunchy and flavorful.

1 SWEET POTATO, FINELY CHOPPED

½ HEAD CAULIFLOWER,
FINELY CHOPPED

1 TABLESPOON COCONUT OIL

1 TEASPOON CHILI POWDER

1 TEASPOON GROUND CUMIN

1 TEASPOON GARLIC POWDER

½ TEASPOON ONION POWDER

1 JALAPEÑO PEPPER,
SEEDED AND DICED

½ SWEET ONION, DICED

¼ CUP FRESH CILANTRO, MINCED

2 CUPS CHERRY TOMATOES, HALVED

JUICE OF 1 LIME, DIVIDED

6 CORN TORTILLAS

¼ CUP ARUGULA

1 AVOCADO, PEELED, PITTED,
AND DICED

1. Preheat the oven to 425°F.

2. In a large bowl, combine the sweet potato and cauliflower, and toss with the coconut oil, chili powder, cumin, garlic powder, and onion powder until well coated.

3. Spread the sweet potato and cauliflower in a single layer on a baking sheet, and bake for 30 minutes.

4. Meanwhile, in a small bowl, combine the jalapeño, onion, cilantro, tomatoes, and half the lime juice. Stir to thoroughly mix the salsa.

5. Shortly before the sweet potato and cauliflower are fully cooked, warm the tortillas in the oven or in a skillet on the stove top for 10 to 15 seconds.

6. Top the tortillas with the arugula, roasted sweet potato and cauliflower, avocado, salsa, and remaining lime juice.

Timesaving tip: *Keep containers with the taco spice seasonings to quickly flavor meals throughout the week.*

Black Bean and Green Chile Enchiladas

SERVES

PREP TIME: **15 MINUTES**   COOK TIME: **40 MINUTES**

Enchiladas are a great make-ahead comfort meal. While most enchilada recipes include cheese, these guys are entirely plant-based and gluten-free. They get their plant-based protein from the black beans. Nutritional yeast is a creative add-in for plant-based dishes because it has a cheese-like flavor, is a complete protein, and contains a variety of B vitamins and zinc. I've included directions for a homemade enchilada sauce to make this dish extra special!

FOR THE SAUCE

1 CUP VEGETABLE BROTH

1 (8-OUNCE) CAN TOMATO SAUCE

3 TABLESPOONS COCONUT OIL

3 TABLESPOONS CHILI POWDER

1 TABLESPOON ARROWROOT POWDER OR CORNSTARCH

2 TEASPOONS GROUND CUMIN

½ TEASPOON ONION POWDER

2 GARLIC CLOVES

FOR THE ENCHILADAS

1 (15-OUNCE) CAN BLACK BEANS, DRAINED AND RINSED

1 CUP SHREDDED CARROTS (OR CARROT PULP)

2 (4-OUNCE) CANS GREEN CHILES

¼ CUP NUTRITIONAL YEAST (OPTIONAL)

6 CORN TORTILLAS

TO MAKE THE SAUCE

1. Preheat the oven to 350°F.

2. In a blender, add the broth, tomato sauce, coconut oil, chili powder, arrowroot powder, cumin, onion powder, and garlic, and blend on high for 30 seconds.

3. In a medium saucepan over low heat, bring the sauce to a simmer, and cook for 5 to 8 minutes, stirring occasionally.

TO MAKE THE ENCHILADAS

1. In a medium bowl, combine the beans, carrots, chiles, and nutritional yeast (if using), and mash together.

2. Scoop some bean mixture evenly onto a tortilla and roll it up. Repeat with the remaining tortillas and bean mixture.

3. Place the rolled tortillas in an ovenproof dish, and pour half the sauce over the top.

4. Cover and bake for 25 minutes.

5. Uncover and add more sauce if desired. Bake, uncovered, for 5 to 8 minutes more.

6. Serve hot with the remaining sauce on the side.

Substitution tip: *If you prefer to use a store-bought sauce, just choose one that's made with real ingredients that you recognize and is not too high in added sugar or sodium.*

Baked Veggie Tots

(MADE WITH JUICE PULP)

SERVES

1

PREP TIME: **10 MINUTES**   COOK TIME: **25 MINUTES**

These tots are not just for kids! Packed with digestion-promoting fiber, these tots are a smart way to use up leftover juice pulp. Try dipping them in mustard and enjoy alongside a big green salad. These savory tots are gluten-free, but you can use any flour you prefer in place of the brown-rice flour (see Substitution Tip).

1 TABLESPOON GROUND FLAXSEED

3 TABLESPOONS WARM
FILTERED WATER

2 TABLESPOONS COCONUT OIL

1 SMALL SWEET POTATO

4 CUPS JUICE PULP
(VEGETABLE PULP WORKS BEST)

3 GARLIC CLOVES, MINCED

1 TEASPOON SEA SALT

½ CUP BROWN-RICE FLOUR

1. Preheat the oven to 425°F.

2. In a small bowl, stir together the flaxseed, and water. Let the mixture sit for 3 minutes.

3. Grate the sweet potato. Wrap the grated potato in a paper towel, squeezing hard to remove all excess liquid.

4. In a large bowl, combine the juice pulp, sweet potato, and garlic, mixing to thoroughly blend.

5. Add the salt, and use a fork to fluff all the ingredients together.

6. While stirring the mixture, slowly sprinkle the brown-rice flour over the vegetables to evenly coat the ingredients.

7. Add the flaxseed mixture and coconut oil to the vegetable mixture, and stir together one last time to thoroughly blend.

8. Scoop spoonfuls of the mixture into the cups of a mini cupcake tin, and bake for 25 minutes.

9. Let cool for 10 minutes before enjoying.

Substitution tip: Brown rice flour is a naturally gluten-free. However, you can substitute the brown-rice flour with coconut flour, almond flour, or tigernut flour. It's important to note that the tot texture may change, depending on the type of flour you use.

Chickpea Beet Burgers

(MADE WITH JUICE PULP)

SERVES

4

PREP TIME: **40 MINUTES**   COOK TIME: **10 MINUTES**

Burgers are a classic food favorite. And this twist on the traditional burger is perfect for those following a plant-based diet, or who simply want to eat healthier! These burger patties contain filling chickpeas, also known as garbanzo beans, for protein, fiber, and energizing carbohydrates. Beets give the burgers a beautiful pink color plus some bonus fiber. The oats are key in this recipe for achieving the right texture and maintaining proper form. These burgers are better baked than grilled. They are also handy to prep, freeze, and enjoy whenever you're ready!

1 CUP ROLLED OATS

3 TABLESPOONS GROUND FLAXSEED

⅓ CUP FILTERED WATER OR BEET JUICE

½ CUP BEET PULP

1 TEASPOON FRESHLY SQUEEZED LIME JUICE

1 (15-OUNCE) CAN CHICKPEAS, DRAINED AND RINSED

1 TEASPOON SEA SALT

1 TEASPOON COCONUT OIL

¼ TEASPOON SMOKED PAPRIKA

4 BURGER BUNS

PICKLES, FOR GARNISH

1. In a food processor or blender, combine the oats and flaxseed. Pulse until the mixture has the consistency of sand.

2. Add the water, beet pulp, and lime juice. Pulse again until well mixed. Let sit for 3 minutes.

3. Add the chickpeas, salt, coconut oil, and paprika, and pulse again until fully blended.

4. Separate the dough into 4 balls and form into patties. Cover and place in the refrigerator for 30 minutes.

5. Preheat the oven to 425°F.

6. Bake the burgers (or sauté in 1 to 2 tablespoons of unrefined coconut oil over medium heat, or grill on high) for 6 minutes on each side or until an internal temperature of 165°F is reached.

7. Serve in a bun, garnished with pickles, greens, and your favorite condiments.

Variation tip: *Instead of beets, feel free to try different pulp options such as carrots or zucchini.*

Rainbow Crunch Veggie Wraps

SERVES

1

PREP TIME: **10 MINUTES**   COOK TIME: **0 MINUTES**

If you're yearning for something a little different and savory, these crunchy wraps make a great light lunch or snack. They are oh-so-good dipped in coconut liquid aminos, which is a soy-free alternative to soy sauce. You could also use the cashew cream sauce from the Loaded Sweet Potatoes (page 172) as a dip.

2 HEADS BUTTER LETTUCE, LEAVES SEPARATED, WASHED AND DRIED

½ AVOCADO, PEELED, PITTED, AND MASHED

2 LARGE CARROTS, THINLY SLICED

½ CUP THINLY SLICED PURPLE CABBAGE

1 CUCUMBER, THINLY SLICED

2 TABLESPOONS CHOPPED SCALLIONS

COCONUT LIQUID AMINOS OR SOY SAUCE, FOR DIPPING

1. On each lettuce leaf, spread a dollop of avocado.

2. Top each leaf with some carrots, cabbage, cucumber, and scallions.

3. Roll up each leaf into a wrap, and serve with coconut liquid aminos for dipping.

Variation tip: *Butter lettuce works exceptionally well as a wrap, but you can also use collard greens or rice paper.*

FRESH OPTIONS

When you start juicing, you may notice that you're buying and using a greater quantity of fresh produce than ever before. It can add up; however, there are a number of ways to save on the cost of produce. Here are some of my favorites.

Shop in season. When you purchase produce in-season, it is at its peak ripeness (and flavor) and will be abundantly available, which means more affordable.

CSA box. A community-supported agriculture (CSA) box is a great way to purchase produce and goods from local farmers. To subscribe to a CSA share program, typically you pay a monthly or yearly subscription fee and you receive shares of the farmer's crops. As you're also cutting out the middleman— the grocery store—making the produce more affordable.

Farmers' market. At a farmers' market you can purchase the freshest foods, while also supporting your local farmers, artisans, and small businesses.

Grow your own garden. Growing your own food takes time and patience, but is incredibly rewarding. Anyone can do it! Plants like zucchini, cucumbers, tomatoes, and herbs are low-maintenance options for new gardeners. If you live in an urban environment, you can grow your garden in pots; just make sure your garden gets at least six to eight hours of quality sunlight each day, and that the pots have drainage holes to prevent waterlog and rot.

10

Super-Simple Snacks

Almond Chia Energy Bites

MAKES

PREP TIME: **10 MINUTES**   SET TIME: **2 HOURS**

These little bites are one part cookie and one part energy bar! This recipe is easily adaptable (see the Variation Tip for adjustment ideas). The dates, however, are essential; they help the ingredients stick together—plus they're rich in iron, fiber, and calcium. Hemp seeds contain omega-3 and omega-6 fats, fiber, and protein—just 3 tablespoons are packed with 10 grams of protein! And chia seeds offer heart-healthy omega-3 fatty acids, fiber, and protein, and their amazing ability to expand in liquid boosts satiety and energy levels.

1 CUP PITTED DATES

½ CUP RAW ALMONDS

¼ CUP HEMP SEEDS

1 TABLESPOON CHIA SEEDS

1 TABLESPOON CACAO POWDER

1 TABLESPOON COCONUT BUTTER

1 TEASPOON GROUND CINNAMON

1 TEASPOON GROUND NUTMEG

1 TEASPOON VANILLA EXTRACT

PINCH SEA SALT

1. In a food processor, combine all the ingredients. Pulse to create a sticky batter.

2. Roll into bite-size balls.

3. Transfer to a container, and freeze for at least 2 hours. Thaw for a few minutes before enjoying.

4. Keep stored in the refrigerator or freezer; they'll keep for about 2 weeks.

Variation tip: *Mix this up to include your favorite health-supportive ingredients. For example, instead of almonds, you can use walnuts, cashews, or pecans.*

Savory Snack Bites

SERVES

PREP TIME: **5 MINUTES**　　　　　SET TIME: **2 HOURS TO OVERNIGHT**

I love making homemade energy bites. The ingredient combinations are endless, and they're a fun way to consume a variety of nourishing whole ingredients. The naturally sweet dates help bind the ingredients together, plus dates are high in minerals such as iron, making them a good natural option for people suffering from anemia. Anemic individuals experience drops in energy levels—and these bites are sure to send sluggishness packing! Store in the refrigerator or freezer for whenever you need that extra boost—they'll keep for about two weeks.

1 CUP PITTED DATES

½ CUP RAW CASHEWS

½ CUP ROLLED OATS

1 TABLESPOON COCONUT OIL

1 TEASPOON CHILI POWDER

PINCH SEA SALT

1. In a food processor, combine all the ingredients. Pulse to create a sticky batter.

2. Roll into bite-size balls.

3. Transfer the balls to a container and freeze for a few hours or overnight.

4. Store in the refrigerator or freezer. If frozen, let them thaw for a few minutes before eating.

Variation tip: *Sweet tooth calling? Cacao powder is delicious added to this recipe for a spicy chocolate treat.*

Honey Cashew Pulp Granola

(MADE WITH JUICE PULP)

SERVES

PREP TIME: **10 MINUTES**   COOK TIME: **8 TO 10 HOURS**

Not much work needed here, just time—so give this granola a go whenever you're home for the day. When selecting honey, look for raw honey, which is pure, unheated, unpasteurized, and unprocessed. Raw local honey has antibacterial properties and also contains energizing B vitamins. If you follow a vegan diet, maple syrup works in place of the honey. I've included options for preparing this recipe in the oven or in a dehydrator—either way will yield a yummy product. Enjoy this granola atop coconut-milk yogurt, in a smoothie bowl, or just as is!

1 CUP PITTED DATES

1 CUP JUICE PULP (BEST FROM FRUITS)

1 CUP ROLLED OATS

1 CUP RAW CASHEWS

1 TABLESPOON RAW LOCAL HONEY

1 TEASPOON SEA SALT

1. If cooking in the oven, preheat the oven to the lowest temperature setting.

2. In a food processor, combine the dates, juice pulp, and oats. Pulse until a sticky, crumbly batter forms. Add the cashews, honey, and salt, and pulse briefly, keeping the batter chunky.

3. To make in a dehydrator, line a dehydrator tray with parchment paper. Spread the granola in an even layer on the tray. Dehydrate for 4 hours. Stir the granola, and dehydrate for a further 4 to 6 hours.

4. To make in the oven, line a baking sheet with parchment paper. Spread the granola in an even layer on the sheet. Bake for 8 hours with the oven door cracked, stirring every hour.

5. Let cool for 10 to 15 minutes before breaking apart. Once cooled, store in an airtight container in the refrigerator. Enjoy within 1 week.

Substitution tip: *If you follow a vegan diet, maple syrup works in place of the honey.*

Variation tip: *Swap out the cashews for pumpkin seeds, almonds, walnuts, or pecans.*

Carrot Coconut Muffins

(MADE WITH JUICE PULP)

SERVES

PREP TIME: **10 MINUTES**   COOK TIME: **25 MINUTES**

Craving some total, guilt-free comfort food? Innovative food substitutes—like egg replacement made from flaxseed—help make gluten- and sugar-free vegan treats possible. The muffins do contain carrot juice pulp, which offers a healthy dose of vitamin C. Blackstrap molasses adds natural sweetness as well as vitamins and minerals such as iron, calcium, magnesium, vitamin B$_6$, and selenium. These tasty treats are dense, hearty, and full of flavor. I love to toast them and enjoy with a little coconut- or almond-butter spread.

2 TABLESPOONS GROUND FLAXSEED

6 TABLESPOONS FILTERED WATER

1 CUP UNSWEETENED ALMOND MILK

¼ CUP COCONUT OIL

1 TEASPOON VANILLA EXTRACT

1 TEASPOON MOLASSES

1 BANANA, PEELED

1 CUP BROWN-RICE FLOUR

1 CUP ALMOND FLOUR

1 CUP COCONUT FLOUR

2 TEASPOONS BAKING SODA

2 TEASPOONS BAKING POWDER

1 TEASPOON GROUND CINNAMON

1 TEASPOON GROUND NUTMEG

1 CUP CARROT JUICE PULP

¼ CUP SHREDDED UNSWEETENED COCONUT

1. Preheat the oven to 350°F. If not using a nonstick muffin pan, grease the muffin cups or line with paper liners.

2. In a small bowl, stir together the flaxseed and water. Let sit for 3 minutes to create a "flax egg."

3. In a blender, combine the almond milk, coconut oil, vanilla, molasses, and banana. Blend until creamy.

4. In a medium bowl, combine the brown-rice flour, almond flour, coconut flour, baking soda, baking powder, cinnamon, and nutmeg. Mix together to blend.

5. Pour the wet ingredients from the blender into the bowl with the dry ingredients. Add the flax egg, and stir all the ingredients together.

6. Fold in the carrot pulp and coconut, mixing together to thoroughly combine.

7. Spoon the batter evenly into the muffin cups.

8. Bake for 25 minutes.

9. Let cool for 5 minutes before enjoying.

Serving tip: *Top with nut, seed, or coconut butter.*

Substitution tip: *Streamline your shopping list—this recipe also works with gluten-free baking mix in place of the brown-rice, almond, and coconut flours.*

Pumpkin Pecan Overnight Oats

SERVES

1

PREP TIME: 5 MINUTES   COOK TIME: 5 MINUTES

With a little prep work, overnight oats are an easy way to enjoy the benefits of oatmeal. You may be surprised to learn that just half a cup of dry rolled oats contains 6 grams of protein. I love pumpkin seeds for this recipe, because they add crunch, texture, and benefits like fiber, iron, and zinc. Zinc boasts antioxidant and anti-inflammatory properties, and helps support hormone health. Enjoy this recipe cold or hot—it's delicious either way.

½ CUP ROLLED OATS

½ CUP UNSWEETENED ALMOND, COCONUT, OR RICE MILK

1 TEASPOON CHIA SEEDS

½ TEASPOON PUMPKIN PIE SPICE, OR MORE TO TASTE

¼ TEASPOON VANILLA EXTRACT

1 TABLESPOON PUMPKIN SEEDS (OR SEED OF CHOICE), FOR TOPPING

1 TABLESPOON PECANS (OR NUT OF CHOICE), FOR TOPPING

¼ CUP BLUEBERRIES (OR BERRY OF CHOICE), FOR TOPPING

1. In a Mason jar, combine the oats, nondairy milk, chia seeds, pumpkin pie spice, and vanilla. Whisk together to blend. Store in the refrigerator overnight.

2. In the morning, give the mixture a stir. The overnight oats should be thick and creamy.

3. Top with the pumpkin seeds, pecans, and blueberries, and enjoy!

Ingredient tip: I recommend using rolled oats in this recipe. Quick oats will yield a mushy texture, and steel-cut oats may be too gritty for some people— but Goldilocks would agree that rolled oats are just right!

Juice-Pulp Crackers

(MADE WITH JUICE PULP)

MAKES

24
CRACKERS

PREP TIME: **10 MINUTES**   COOK TIME: **1 TO 6 HOURS**

Salty or sweet? I'll go with salty! I love crunchy, salty crackers, and they're even better dipped in a delicious spread like hummus or gua-camole. To be honest, these juice crackers take a little work, but if you're a cracker addict like me, they're worth it. Plus, they're a fun way to get your crunch fix while you repurpose juice pulp, prevent food waste, and nourish your body with additional plant-powered ingredients. If you're using a dehydrator with multiple trays, make multiple batches! If you don't have a dehydrator, you can bake the crackers (see Cooking Tip).

2 CUPS CARROT PULP (OR OTHER JUICING PULP OR PULP BLEND; SEE SUBSTITUTION TIP)

½ CUP GROUND FLAXSEED

1 TEASPOON SEA SALT

½ TEASPOON FRESHLY GROUND BLACK PEPPER

½ TEASPOON GARLIC POWDER

¼ TEASPOON ONION POWDER

¼ CUP FILTERED WATER, PLUS MORE IF NECESSARY

1. In a large bowl, combine the carrot pulp, flaxseed, salt, pepper, garlic powder, and onion powder. Mix well.

2. While mixing, add the water 1 tablespoon at a time. Depending on how dry the pulp is, you may need a bit less water or a little more. Mix until the dough becomes a slightly sticky ball that will not crumble.

3. On a parchment paper–lined dehydrator tray, spread the cracker dough into an even layer about ⅛ inch thick. Score the dough with a sharp knife; the cut lines will help break the crackers apart later.

4. Place the dough in the dehydrator at 120°F for about 4 hours. Depending on your dough mixture and the dehydrator you use, the crackers may take more or less time. Check on them every hour to reach your desired crunchiness.

Cooking tip: *If you don't have a dehydrator, you can dry the crackers out in a preheated 300°F oven for 1 to 2 hours. After 45 minutes, check them every 15 minutes to prevent burning.*

Substitution tip: *If you don't want to use carrot pulp, pulp from dark leafy greens and beets makes excellent crackers.*

White Bean Lemon Hummus and Carrots

MAKES

SERVINGS

PREP TIME: **5 MINUTES**   COOK TIME: **0 MINUTES**

Homemade hummus is really easy to make, and when made from white beans, it's full of protein and fiber. This dip also contains garlic, a super-beneficial and antibacterial ninja! Garlic is known to be heart-healthy and support a strong immune system. FYI, for this plan, you can buy store-bought hummus if you prefer. I'm a big fan of convenience items, especially if these shortcuts help you eat healthier. But if you're up for it, this recipe makes multiple servings, perfect to enjoy throughout the week or share with friends and family.

1 (15-OUNCE) CAN WHITE BEANS, DRAINED AND RINSED

¼ CUP OLIVE OIL

2 TABLESPOONS TAHINI

2 GARLIC CLOVES

JUICE OF 1 LEMON

½ TEASPOON GROUND CUMIN

½ TEASPOON PAPRIKA

¼ TEASPOON SEA SALT

¼ TEASPOON FRESHLY GROUND BLACK PEPPER

1. Combine all the ingredients in a food processor and pulse until creamy.

2. Serve alongside baby carrots, celery, bell peppers, or cucumbers for dipping.

3. Keep stored in the refrigerator, and enjoy within 1 week.

Ingredient tip: *When selecting store-bought hummus, aim for organic.*

Guacamole with Cucumber Chips

MAKES

2

SERVINGS

PREP TIME: **5 MINUTES**   COOK TIME: **0 MINUTES**

I'll be honest: Cucumber "chips" are not as delicious as potato chips! The real star of this snack is the guacamole. The cucumber chips are purely a way to eat more guacamole, but you can feel good binge-ing on them knowing that cucumbers are hydrating, low in sodium, and contain B vitamins, vitamin K, and vitamin C. For this rec-ipe, you'll want ripe, fresh avocados, which are a heart-healthy and nutrient-dense fruit. In fact, avocados are one of the only fruits that contain good-for-you monounsaturated fats. Enjoy this savory, sati-ating, and energy-boosting snack.

1 RIPE AVOCADO, PEELED, PITTED, AND SLICED

JUICE OF 1 LEMON

¼ TEASPOON SEA SALT

1 OR 2 CUCUMBERS, CUT INTO THIN ROUNDS

1. In a medium bowl, mash the avocado.

2. Add the lemon juice and salt, and mix together until evenly blended.

3. Serve with the cucumbers or your favorite fresh vegetables for dipping.

Ingredient tip: *For extra crunch, use baby cucumbers.*

Fruit Leathers

(MADE WITH JUICE PULP)

SERVES

PREP TIME: **5 MINUTES**   COOK TIME: **3 TO 4 HOURS**

Fruit leathers are not just for kids! This homemade version contains no processed sugars, because they are made with real ingredients—strawberries, lemon, honey, and apple juice pulp. They also contain fiber and vitamin C, and they taste delicious! This recipe is a great way to repurpose juice pulp into another tasty treat the whole family will go wild over.

2 CUPS STRAWBERRIES

1 CUP APPLE JUICE PULP

1 TABLESPOON RAW LOCAL HONEY

JUICE OF ½ LEMON

1. Preheat the oven to 250°F.

2. Line a baking sheet with parchment paper.

3. In a blender, combine all the ingredients and blend on high for 1 minute.

4. On the baking sheet, spread the mixture as evenly and thinly as possible.

5. Place in the oven for 3 hours, or in a dehydrator at 115°F for 4 hours.

6. Once cooked, let the fruit sit for 1 hour.

7. Carefully peel the fruit off the tray, cut into strips, roll up, and enjoy!

Substitution tip: *This recipe is easy to adapt; you can use blueberries or raspberries instead of strawberries, or try pear in place of the apple.*

Cinnamon Banana Cacao Chia Pudding

SERVES

1

PREP TIME: **5 MINUTES**   SET TIME: **10 MINUTES**

A guiltless answer to your nagging sweet tooth! Raw cacao powder is nutrient-dense and loaded with antioxidants. It is harvested similarly to cocoa powder, but cocoa powder is typically sweetened and processed at high temperatures, which can denature nutrients and antioxidants. Raw cacao powder is dried and processed at low temperatures, preserving more nutrients.

1 CUP UNSWEETENED ALMOND MILK

3 TABLESPOONS CHIA SEEDS

1 TABLESPOON RAW CACAO POWDER

1 TEASPOON MAPLE SYRUP

½ TEASPOON CINNAMON

½ MEDIUM, RIPE BANANA, SLICED, FOR TOPPING

1 TABLESPOON RAW ALMONDS, FOR TOPPING

1 TEASPOON COCOA NIBS, FOR TOPPING (OPTIONAL)

1. In a small bowl, whisk together the almond milk, chia seeds, cacao powder, maple syrup, and cinnamon. Let sit for at least 10 minutes, or cover and store in the refrigerator overnight.

2. Stir before enjoying, then top with the banana slices, almonds, and cacao nibs (if using), and enjoy!

Substitution tip: *Raw local honey or liquid stevia are great natural sweetener options in place of maple syrup.*

Resources

THE BIG BOOK OF JUICES
NATALIE SAVONA
Looking for more juice recipes?
This book has over 400 simple juice
and smoothie recipes to explore.

BLENDTEC
www.blendtec.com
Blendtec is a high-speed blender
I strongly recommend. The Blendtec website is also a great place for
recipe inspiration.

ENVIRONMENTAL
WORKING GROUP
www.ewg.org
If you're interested in eating more
organic fruits and vegetables, or
even just learning more about the
foods you're putting in your body,
the Environmental Working Group
website is a great resource. The EWG
tests produce for pesticide residue
and is the creator of the Dirty Dozen
and Clean Fifteen lists (page 24).

HEALTH NUT NUTRITION
www.healthnutnutrition.ca
Recommended website featuring healthy food recipes with
Nikole Goncalves.

HEALTHY GROCERY GIRL
www.healthygrocerygirl.com
Easy and delicious plant-based
recipes, videos, and meal plans. This
is my website, so I may be biased,
but I think it's a pretty great resource!

KRIS CARR
www.kriscarr.com
Kris Carr is an inspirational wellness
advocate and juicing expert. Her
website and books are wonderful
resources for anyone who wants to
eat more plants, as well as nurture
and care for total well-being.

MIND BODY GREEN
www.mindbodygreen.com
Recommended website for
whole-body wellness inspiration
and education.

OMEGA JUICER

www.omegajuicers.com
The Omega is one of my favorite home juicers, and the company website has great information and recipe inspirations.

PRESSED JUICERY

www.pressedjuicery.com
If I'm pressed for time (pun intended!), one of my favorite juice shops is Pressed Juicery. It provides delicious cold-pressed juices, and their FREEZE soft-serve made from fruits, veggies, and nuts is incredible.

SIMPLY QUINOA

www.simplyquinoa.com
Recommended website featuring plant-powered recipes with Alyssa Rimmer.

SUPERFOOD JUICES & SMOOTHIES
TINA LEIGH, CHHC

This book has 100 delicious and nutritious recipes made with a variety of popular superfoods. It also provides an in-depth look into the history and health benefits of various superfoods.

SWEET POTATO SOUL

www.sweetpotatosoul.com
Recommended website featuring vegan recipes with Jenné Claiborne.

THE TOASTED PINE NUT

www.thetoastedpinenut.com
Recommended website featuring gorgeous, mostly gluten-free recipes with Lindsay.

VITAMIX

www.vitamix.com
A high-speed blender like the Vitamix is a fantastic kitchen staple for creamy, plant-powered blended juices and smoothies. The Vitamix site also has great recipe ideas.

WEELICIOUS

www.weelicious.com
Recommended website featuring easy, family-friendly recipes with Catherine McCord.

References

Akilen, R., Tsiami, A., Devendra, D., and Robinson, N. "Glycated Haemoglobin and Blood Pressure–Lowering Effect of Cinnamon in Multi-Ethnic Type 2 Diabetic Patients in the UK: A Randomized, Placebo-Controlled, Double-Blind Clinical Trial." October 27, 2010. PubMed.gov. Accessed September 4, 2017. www.ncbi.nlm.nih.gov/pubmed/20854384.

Calbom, Cherie. *The Juice Lady's Guide To Juicing For Health.* New York, NY: Penguin Group, 2008.

Centers for Disease Control and Prevention. "National Report on Human Exposure to Environmental Chemicals." Accessed July 17, 2017. www.cdc.gov/exposurereport.

Feskanich, D., Ziegler, R.G., Michaud, D.S., Giovannucci, E.L., Speizer, F.E., Willett, W.C., and Colditz, G.A. "Prospective Study of Fruit and Vegetable Consumption and Risk of Lung Cancer Among Men and Women." November 15, 2000. PubMed.gov. Accessed September 4, 2017. www.ncbi.nlm.nih.gov/pubmed/11078758.

Fruits & Veggies More Matters. "Dietary Guidelines for Americans: Key Highlights." Accessed July 9, 2017. www.fruitsandveggiesmorematters.org/dietary-guidelines-for-americans.

He, F.J. and MacGregor, G.A. "Beneficial Effects of Potassium on Human Health." August, 2008. PubMed.gov. Accessed September 4, 2017. www.ncbi.nlm.nih.gov/pubmed/18724413.

Mayo Clinic. "Dietary Fiber: Essential For A Healthy Diet." Accessed September 4, 2017. www.mayoclinic.org/healthy-lifestyle/nutrition-and-healthy-eating/in-depth/fiber/art-20043983.

Murillo, G. and Mehta, R.G. "Cruciferous Vegetables and Cancer Prevention." June 22, 2011. PubMed.gov. Accessed September 4, 2017. www.ncbi.nlm.nih.gov/pubmed/12094621.

Nielsen, S.E., et al. "Effect of Parsley (Petroselinum Crispum) Intake On Urinary Apigenin Excretion, Blood Antioxidant Enzymes and Biomarkers for Oxidative Stress In Human Subjects." PubMed.gov. Accessed July 19, 2017. www.ncbi.nlm.nih.gov/pubmed/10615220.

Omura, Y. and Beckman, S.L. "Role of Mercury (Hg) In Resistant Infections & Effective Treatment of Chlamydia Trachomatis and Herpes Family Viral Infections (and Potential Treatment For Cancer) by Removing Localized Hg Deposits with Chinese Parsley and Delivering Effective Antibiotics Using Various Drug Uptake Enhancement Methods." Accessed July 19, 2017. www.ncbi.nlm.nih.gov/pubmed/8686573.

Quigley, Eamonn M.M. "Gut Bacteria in Health and Disease." Accessed September 4, 2017. www.ncbi.nlm.nih.gov/pmc/articles/PMC3983973.

Schwalfenberg, Gerry K. "The Alkaline Diet: Is There Evidence That an Alkaline pH Diet Benefits Health?" Accessed September 4, 2017. www.ncbi.nlm.nih.gov/pmc/articles/PMC3195546/#B1a.

Sharma, V., Kansai, L., and Sharma, A. "Prophylactic Efficacy of Coriandrum Sativum (Coriander) on Testis of Lead-Exposed Mice." September, 2010. PubMed.gov. Accessed September 4, 2017. www.ncbi.nlm.nih.gov/pubmed/19902160.

Soltani, M., Khosravi, A.R., Asadi, F., and Shokri, H. "Evaluation of Protective Efficacy of Spirulina Platensis in Balb/C Mice with Candidiasis." December 22, 2012. PubMed.gov. Accessed September 4, 2017. www.ncbi.nlm.nih.gov/pubmed/23518167.

United States Department of Agriculture. "Dietary Guidelines for Americans 2015–2020." Accessed September 4, 2017. www.choosemyplate.gov/dietary-guidelines.

Waugh, Anne and Allison Grant. *Anatomy and Physiology in Health and Illness, 10th edition*. Philadelphia, PA: Churchill Livingstone Elsevier, 2007.

Recipe Index

Index

Acknowledgements

Thank you so much to the Callisto Media team for inviting me to author this book, and for being such a joy to work with! Thank you to my husband, Aaron, for taking on extra work projects for our business and around the house while I wrote this book, and for helping drink all the fresh juices during recipe testing! I also would like to thank my parents, my family, friends, our Healthy Grocery Girl® team member Jeni and the HGG community for your ongoing love and support. Last but not least, a big thanks to God, for opening new doors and providing me with opportunities such as this book. Cheers with a big glass of fresh, cold-pressed juice!

About the Author

Megan Roosevelt, RDN, is a registered dietitian nutritionist, producer, host, and founder of Healthy Grocery Girl®. Her realistic, fun, and genuine approach to healthy living has enabled her to cultivate a loyal online following and community at HealthyGroceryGirl.com, on YouTube, and on Instagram.

Healthy Grocery Girl® is a wellness website and video-production company helping busy people and families enjoy real food and natural living. Healthy Grocery Girl® keeps it simple and fun with weekly blogs, videos, and an online wellness membership providing nutrition programs, video courses, and shopping guides. It is the No. 1 Family-Friendly Dietitian Channel on YouTube with millions of total views.

Megan is also an internationally published author and nutrition expert for television and magazines. She lives in sunny Los Angeles, California, with her husband and business partner, Aaron Roosevelt.

Visit Megan Online:

www.HealthyGroceryGirl.com

YouTube: YouTube.com/HealthyGroceryGirl

Instagram: @HealthyGroceryGirl